# THE LAST GIANT OF BERINGIA

*The Mystery of the Bering Land Bridge*

DAN O'NEILL

A Member of the Perseus Books Group
New York

Hardcover first published in 2004 by Westview Press, A Member of the Perseus Books Group. Paperback first published in 2005 by Basic Books.

Books published by Basic Books are available at special discounts for bulk purchases in the United States by corporations, institutions, and other organizations. For more information, please contact the Special Markets Department at the Perseus Books Group, 11 Cambridge Center, Cambridge, MA 02142, or call (617) 252-5298, (800) 255-1514 or email special.markets@perseusbooks.com.

A Cataloging-in-Publication data record for this book is available from the Library of Congress.

HC: ISBN-13 978-0-8133-4197-2; ISBN 0-8133-4197-3.
PBK: ISBN-13 978-0-465-05157-1; ISBN 0-465-05157-X

The paper used in this publication meets the requirements of the American National Standard for Permanence of Paper for Printed Library Materials Z39.48–1984.

Typeface used in this text: Times

10 9 8 7 6 5 4 3 2

# THE LAST GIANT OF BERINGIA

Hopkins' 1948 field crew amid grassy hummocks and dead willow near Imuruk Lake, Seward Peninsula, Alaska. Left is probably Bob Sigafoos; the others (with mosquito headnets) are probably Art Fernald and Jim Seitz
*(Photo by Dave Hopkins, courtesy of Dana Hopkins)*

For Sarah

# Contents

# 1

# THE TOAST OF KHABAROVSK

West to east, from the Ural Mountains on the edge of Europe to the Sea of Japan, the Trans-Siberian Railroad straddles a quarter of the globe. It runs across the Barabiniskaya Steppe and into the taiga, skirting Lake Baikal to the south and Manchuria to the north. One raw spring day during the Cold War, a train carrying scientists clattered east along this great thoroughfare. All across the breadth of the Soviet Union, the train stopped to collect technical specialists, all bound for Khabarovsk on the Amur River, the line's farthest east stop. There it heaved a steamy sigh, and the scientists climbed down to the platform and into waiting taxis. On the road into town, cabs from the station merged with cabs from the airport, all carrying scientists, some from as far away as Western Europe and North America. By nightfall hundreds of scientists from around the world had converged at the old hotel on the town square.

Khabarovsk in 1973 was both rustic town and modern city. Most of the buildings on the square were modern, if blocky and utilitarian. But beyond a radius of a couple blocks, a visitor inclined to stroll found log cabins and outhouses. On warm days when the wind was right, he could detect the latter before descending the hotel steps.

At Khabarovsk, Siberia, in 1973 (right photo), Hopkins stands between his Russian counterpart, Beringian geologist Oleg Petrov, and Rosa Gitterman, a Pleistocene pollen analysis expert. Encouraged by Hopkins since his student days, Russian paleoecologist Andrei Sher (left photo) became Hopkins' collaborator and one of his closest personal friends *(Photos courtesy of Andrei Sher)*

On this particular evening, the hotel shone with lights as the darkness gathered, and the scientists assembled in the main banquet hall. The dinner party livened as vodka flowed and first one, then another Russian rose to toast political rivals united by science. Everyone got into the spirit. The Hungarians drank to the Czechs; the Czechs saluted the Finns. The East Germans hailed the West Germans, who cheered the Americans, who started the Russians going again. All around the room, bottles clanked noisily on the rims of eight-ounce water glasses, and the revelers tossed off vodka shots chased with champagne. Then one of the Russians started a kind of chant. Others joined in. Quickly it rolled through the room. Feet began to stomp and heavy glasses banged down on the tables. It grew more boisterous and polyglot as every flushed face took it up, a dozen accents calling out HOP-KINS-HOP-KINS-HOP-KINS. And it did not end until a shy, fifty-one-year-old California geologist, wearing longish hair and red pants, pushed his plastic glasses back on his nose and, with reluctance, stood.

Hopkins does not remember the moment, but archeologist Jim Dixon remembers it as if it were yesterday. It *would* be memorable, says Dixon, if you were a young graduate student, not one of the elite invitees, and had wangled an invitation to the Khabarovsk conference by calling up the renowned Hopkins cold and pleading to be included. "It was impressive. I was very much awed by the greatness of Hopkins, and by the Russians' love for the guy." When the proceedings were compiled into a book, conference chairman V. L. Kontrimavichus introduced it with special reference to Hopkins: "I thank Dr. Hopkins for coming to Khabarovsk for the symposium and for maintaining correspondence later. I thank this great scientist, who is a pioneer and great enthusiast in the study of Bering Land and a great friend of all the Soviet geologists working on Bering Land."

May 1973. Early spring, too, in the incipient thaw in Cold War relations between the Soviet Union and the United States. The two governments were beginning to discover what their Northern scientists had already begun to prove: that they had common ground. Literally. Hopkins called it Beringia.

Beringia (Beh-RIN-gee-a) is the name given to the Bering Land Bridge, the surmised ancient dry land connection between North America and Asia, and to the adjacent then exposed lands, roughly between the Mackenzie River in Canada's Northwest Territories and the Kolyma (or even as far west as the Lena) River in Siberia. But did this hypothetical land bridge really exist? If so, when? What sort of climate prevailed there? Could plants grow so far north during the Ice Age? And could that probably sparse vegetation sustain the gigantic mammals of the Pleistocene—the woolly mammoth and the giant short-faced bear? Finally, can knowledge of this ecological picture, along with archeology, answer a further question—*the* question—debated for centuries: Did Asian hunters, equipped with skin sewing technology and expertly crafted stone-tipped weapons pursue the drifting aggregations of herbivores north and east across the land bridge and into North America? And were these hunters who passed through Beringia the first to enter not just a new continent, but the back side of the world, an entire hemisphere of the planet never before seen by man?

Though the first Americans' discovery and colonization of half of the earth is one of the great accomplishments in human history, it has been all but overshadowed by disputes as to *how* they did it and *who* exactly they were. This debate over the last great migration of the human species, now running for more than four hundred years, has become one of the most rancorous and enduring controversies in all of science.

The story speaks to a more recent and more pressing scientific question as well. The ancient history of this Northern Atlantis (its climate shifts, the record of species exchanges across the land bridge, and the cause of the extinctions of most of the large animals) all may offer clues as to how Northern

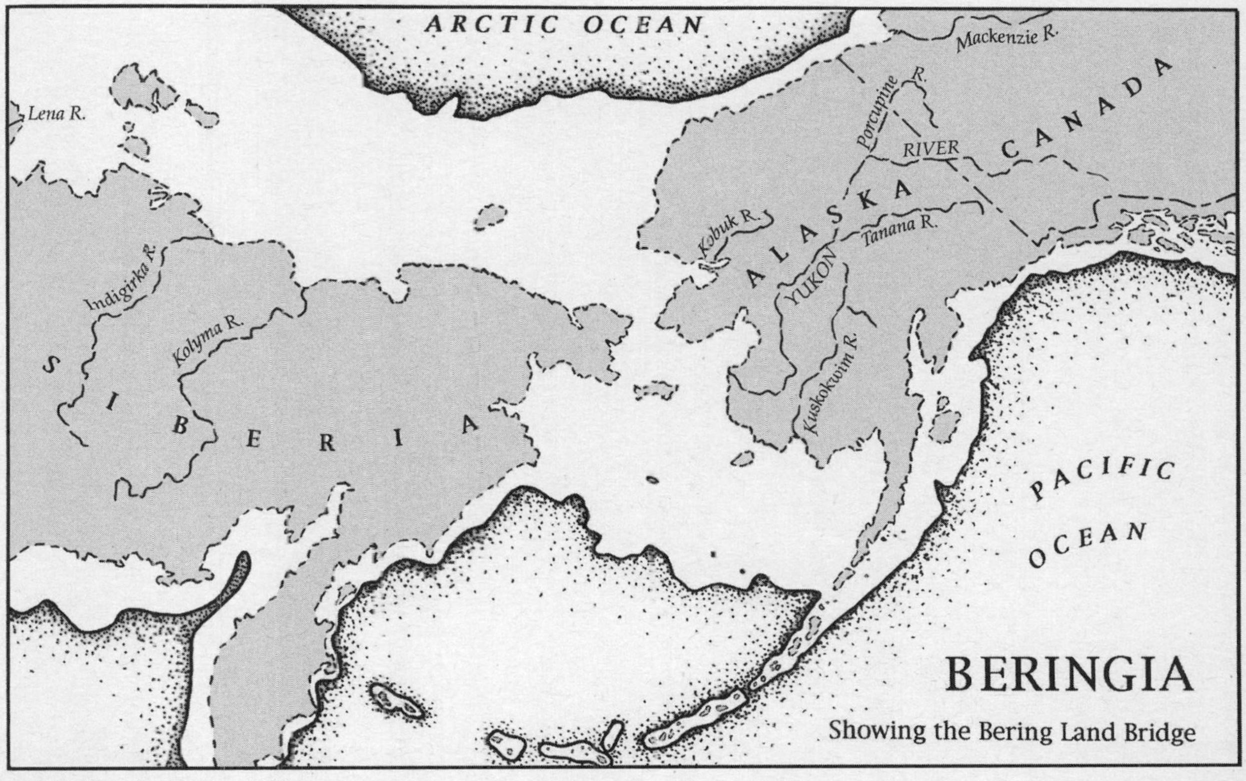


D. O'Neill (After Hopkins, 1982)

ecosystems will respond to global climate change in the future. Greenhouse warming attributable to human activities is expected to show its greatest effects in the Arctic. In fact, it seems to be happening now.

Fray Jose de Acosta, a Jesuit missionary, first advanced the land bridge theory in 1590. Early Spanish settlers and other European thinkers had difficulty explaining the indigenous people. The Bible had not mentioned them, unless, of course, they were the Lost Tribes of Israel. Perhaps the answer was that they weren't human at all, but had spontaneously generated from mud. That notion had the advantage of making the subsequent enslavement of the natives a less disquieting moral issue. Some speculated that the new land must be Plato's Atlantis and the people Atlanteans. Those who liked to draw on the known to explain the unknown suggested the Indians looked to have the blended blood of Scandinavians, Ethiopians, Chinese, and Indonesians. Others thought, no, the mix seemed more Scythian, with a pinch of Spanish, Welsh, and Polynesian. Even the American Puritan Cotton Mather found the time (after the witch trials reached satisfactory conclusions) to weigh in. In 1702 he wrote, "probably the Devil decoyed these miserable savages hither, in hopes that the gospel of the lord Jesus Christ would never come here to destroy or disturb his absolute empire over them."

But in 1590 Acosta, who had by then been working among the Indians of Mexico and Peru for sixteen years, published a work of natural history that dismissed theories involving Atlantis, Chinese Norsemen, or the animation of mud. As a good friar, he took it as fact that man had not evolved in situ in the New World. Adam and Eve, after all, had been created in the Old World, so man had to have migrated to the new one. Acosta considered transoceanic travel but decided the possibility unlikely. He concluded that the solution to the problem must lie in the as yet unknown northern latitudes. Writing nearly one hundred fifty years before the discovery of the Bering Strait, the wise priest speculated that when explorers ventured into the upper reaches of North America, they would find that the Old and New Worlds were either "continued and joined with the other," as the two American continents were, or that "they approach on neerer unto another" across a narrow water gap that would not greatly inhibit migration.

When he addressed the issue of animal migration, particularly of the smaller beasts, Acosta thought overland travel a more likely explanation than their having swum even a short stretch of ocean. He further theorized that the human occupation of the Americas was less a migration, per se, than a gradual expansion accomplished "without consideration in changing by little and little their lands and habitations. Some peopling the lands they found, and other seeking for newe, in time they came to inhabit the Indies." Similarities between the indigenous people of the Americas and Asian peoples seemed obvious, and the notion of a land connection was generally accepted thereafter.

Until 1728. On a foggy day in that year, Vitus Bering sailed through the strait later named for him, proving that no landmass connected North America to Asia. Had the day been clear, Bering and his men would have beheld one continent to starboard and another to port. And had he tossed a sounding line overboard, it would have told the rest of the story.

Like lines of longitude gathering at the North Pole, several lines of reasoning converged on the hypothesis of a northern migration route to the New World. In 1778, Captain James Cook sailed through Bering Strait, noting that only a short reach of sea separated the continents, and convincing many that this was the point of entry for the first Americans. In 1887, a geologist named Angelo Heilprin noticed that a comparison of Old and New World animal species showed they were quite dissimilar in southern latitudes, more alike in midlatitudes, and nearly identical in the north. This strongly suggested that, if species diversification was a function of distance from the north, then the species must have dispersed from that direction. A few years later another geologist, George Dawson, observed that the seas separating Alaska and Siberia are shallow and "must be considered physiographically as belonging to the continental plateau region as distinct from that of the ocean basins proper." Dawson suggested that "more than once and perhaps during prolonged periods [there existed] a wide terrestrial plain connecting North America and Asia." His idea was that earth movements or continental uplift had periodically established or submerged the connection.

Then, in 1892, mammoth bones showed up on the Pribilof Islands, three hundred miles from the Alaska mainland. Either these giant hairy elephants were awfully good swimmers, or the islands were once high spots in a broad plain, conjunct south to north with the entire Alaskan and Siberian landmasses. A Canadian geologist named W. A. Johnson added the final theoretical puzzle piece. In 1934, Johnson made the connection between fluctuations in sea levels and past periods of glaciation. "During the Wisconsin stage of glaciation," he wrote, "the general level of the sea must have been lower owing to the accumulation of ice on the land. The amount of lowering is generally accepted to be at least 180 feet, so that a land bridge probably existed during the height of the last glaciation ... ." At about the same time, Eric Hultén described his theories of a vast, largely unglaciated lowland that served as a refuge for plants and animals during the Ice Age. Naming the land Beringia, Hultén supposed it had been the terrestrial route taken by humans into the New World. That was the state of scientific understanding in the late 1940s when Hopkins turned his attention to the problem.

At Khabarovsk in 1973, Hopkins was only halfway through a fifty-year study of the Bering Land Bridge. Nonetheless, he was already the world's leading authority. For half a century, scientists from a range of disciplines would orbit Hopkins and the core of scientific understanding that he amassed. Like comets hurtling into dark regions of space, they would inevitably loop back to him, drawn by his gravity, glowing with the results of their voyage. And, reenergized by proximity to him, they would blaze outward again into as yet unlit regions of the past.

# 2
# The Ice Age

The Pleistocene Epoch, commonly called the Ice Age, began about 1.75 million years ago. It ended just ten thousand years ago, though some scientists think we are still in it, merely enjoying an "interglacial" reprieve—a day at the beach in geologic time. During this period, the climate was not uniformly cold, but fluctuated in great cycles. Warming trends followed cooling ones, sometimes oscillating in periods of tens to hundreds of thousands of years. In the most recent of these cold cycles, temperatures fell starting about twenty-eight thousand* years ago and continued falling until perhaps eighteen thousand years ago. Brutally cold conditions, unlike anything known on the planet today, locked down on the polar regions and the adjacent latitudes. The effect was greater in the Northern Hemisphere owing to peculiarities of weather patterns and ocean currents, which owed in turn to the direction of the earth's rotation, differences in the distribution of land and sea, and irregularities in the earth's orbit. In colder regions, more snow fell in the winter than melted in the summer. So, it accumulated. It built up in layers that melted slightly, condensed and recrystallized. Each new season's snowfall compressed the layers beneath it. The result: masses of glacial ice.

*Dates in this book are given in radiocarbon years, which, while they do not correspond exactly with calendar years, are close enough and are the standard terms of reference in virtually all writing on the topic.

Year after year, glaciers thickened until the leading edges pushed out over the land, merging with one another. The Laurentide Ice Sheet, the largest in North America, piled up to a height of nearly two miles. Centered on Hudson Bay, it grew to cover practically all of what is today Canada. It joined with the Greenland Ice Sheet to the east, and plowed its way south nearly as far as what is now the state of Kentucky. At some points, the Laurentide Ice Sheet likely joined North America's other great mass of ice, the three-thousand-mile-long Cordilleran Ice Sheet, which draped itself along the coastal mountains of western North America from Puget Sound to the Aleutian archipelago. Advancing ice also blanketed Northern Europe, scattered parts of Asia, the world's principal mountain ranges, and, of course, Antarctica. Amazingly, glaciers did not penetrate Interior Alaska, where relatively arid conditions inhibited their development.

Where the ice floated on the sea, as pack ice and icebergs, it did not affect sea level. A floating iceberg displaces the same quantity of water that the berg would produce if liquefied. But most of the world's ice was not floating. It sat ensconced on the land and so did affect sea level. Evaporation continued to remove water from the sea, the winds transporting clouds of it over the land, where it fell as precipitation, often snow. Some of this returned to the oceans via the rivers during the cool summer, but much of it remained on the land as ice. Ice sheets held roughly one-twentieth of all the world's water, half of that in the Laurentide Ice Sheet alone. Consequently, the sea fell during the Ice Ages, eventually dropping an estimated one hundred twenty-five meters, or about four hundred feet below its present level.

As the sea receded, the shapes of the continents changed. The eastern seaboard of North America gained real estate as the shoreline migrated hundreds of miles east to the edge of the

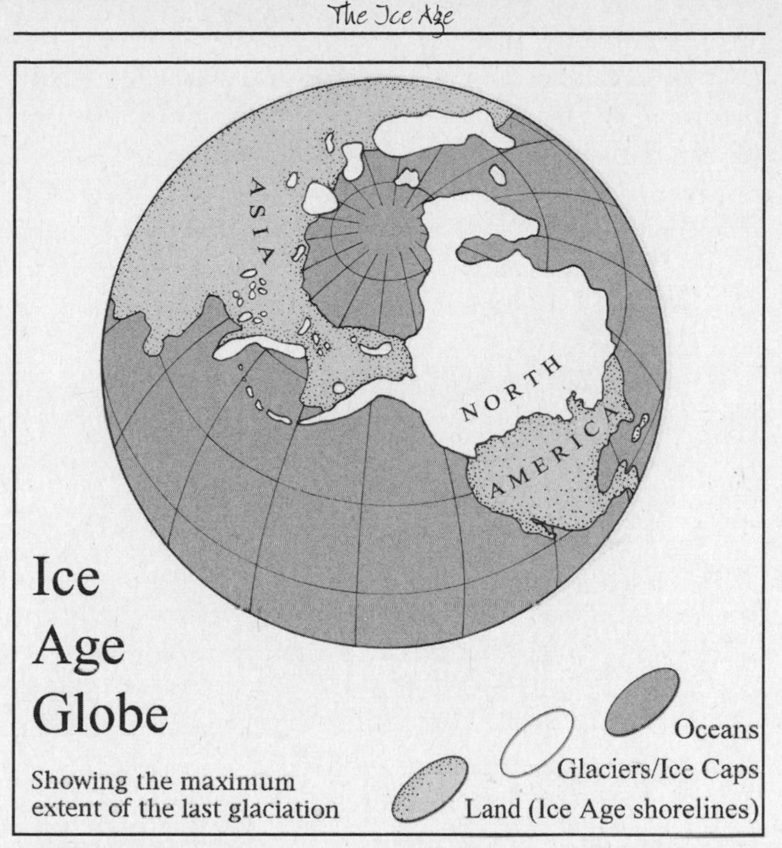


D. O'Neill (after Dixon, 1993)

outer continental shelf. On the Pacific side, the coastline did not change as noticeably because the continental shelf does not extend very far offshore. But north of the North Pacific, in the region of Bering Sea, a shallow continental shelf stretched continuously from Alaska to Siberia. And as the sea pulled away from the shore, Asia and North America began to reach for each other like the outstretched arms of God and Adam on the ceiling of the Sistine Chapel. When the finger tips touched, a charge of new life streamed into the Americas.

Not all at once, of course. During the most recent glaciation, the first linkup probably occurred with a continuous strip of land running from Siberia's Cape Chaplin, through St. Lawrence Island to the southern part of Norton Sound. But temperatures—and therefore the sea level—continued to fall. The shelf broadened until perhaps eighteen thousand years ago, the height of glacial activity. Then the continental shelf between Alaska and Siberia stood proud of the water for over nine hundred miles, north to south, encompassing the Alaska Peninsula to the south and extending beyond Wrangell Island to the north. North America and Asia were joined at the head like great, sprawling Siamese twins.

For Alaska, the effect was extreme, and it involved much more than a strip of land that permitted overland passage between two continents. With each appearance and disappearance of the Bering Land Bridge, Alaska essentially switched continental allegiances. When it was joined with Asia during the cold cycles, it was perforce cut off from the rest of North America by the very glaciers that had lowered the sea. Then, as a matter of biogeographical reality, Alaska became part of Northeast Asia. During the warm cycles, however, the glaciers melted, causing the seas to rise and the land bridge to flood. With a water barrier in place to the west, and no glacial barrier to the east and south, Alaska again became a province of North America. She was like a fickle lover: when times were warm, she accepted North America's embrace; but when the air grew cold, she reached for Asia.

Traditionally, scientists thought that there were four Ice Ages in the Cenozoic, the current era, extending back about seventy million years. American scientists have named them after states: the Wisconsin, Illinoian, Kansan, and Nebraskan. And between each of these came a warmer, interglacial period they have called, respectively, the Sangamon, Yarmouth, and Aftonian. In Northern Europe, scientists working in the Alps named the four corresponding glaciations there after rivers that flow out of the Alps into the Danube: the Würm, Riss, Mindel, and Gunz. To help keep things crystal clear, researchers from Britain, Northern Germany/Holland, Poland, European Russia, and Siberia have all offered terminology of different partisan provenience. Hence, the last glacial stage is variously known as the Wisconsin, Würm, Monastirian, Devensian, Weichselian, Vistulian, Valdaian, Sarta, and Ermakavo.

By the 1960s, however, drilling records were showing many more glacial tills than just those four. In the 1970s, deep-sea drilling yielded unambiguous evidence for as many as sixteen glacial stages, separated by interglacials, during the last million years or so. The Bering Land Bridge would have connected the continents during each of the glacials, as soon as the sea level fell to about one hundred sixty feet below the present level, while the Bering Strait seaway would have existed during all or most of the interglacials, whenever sea levels rose higher than minus one hundred sixty feet. The exact number of appearances of the land bridge might not be known for a long time.

Of particular interest to Beringian scholars is the last land bridge, which existed at least during the extremely cold period between roughly twenty-five thousand and fourteen thousand years ago (but which may have remained in place more or less continuously through the last interglacial, when sea levels oscillated around the breech point). Great circumpolar plains extended from southern Europe into central Asia, east to Siberia, and across the land bridge into the middle of Alaska. Much of these interior regions, like Interior Alaska, escaped glaciation throughout the Ice Ages because mountains or distances impeded the migration of coastal moisture, inhibiting the snowfall necessary for glaciers to develop. But even if largely free of glaciers, Beringia was still a harsh place, dry and windy. Loess (windblown glacial silt) filled the air and piled up in shifting dunes. The vegetative cover may have been sparse, the land a polar desert, a drier version of today's tundra intermittently established on frozen silt.

Notwithstanding these extremes, Beringia seemed to have supported a great bestiary, more impressive even than its modern African counterparts. Woolly mammoths ranged throughout Beringia, protected from the icy winds by six-inch-thick hairy coats hanging in long skirts. From their domed heads fifteen feet in the air, massive tusks up to thirteen feet long curved and recurved like an art nouveau motif. Ground sloths, torpid behemoths that could attain six thousand pounds, nonetheless displayed wicked claws and teeth. The long-horned and probably fierce steppe bison might have stood as tall at the shoulder as a smallish mammoth. Alongside the forlorn looking faces of muskoxen, broad horns dropped down and terminated in little flips, like the starched caps of Dutchwomen. From a distance, with their humps, rumps, and swaybacks, they looked like double haystacks. On the run, with their guard hair reaching nearly to the ground and all but obscuring their short legs, they seemed to fly over the tundra as if they were riding magic carpets. Horses evolved in North America and crossed the land bridge into Asia (and a good thing they did, because their New World populations were totally extinguished, until European explorers brought their descendants back aboard sailing ships). The saiga antelope, a goatlike antelope with a greatly enlarged muzzle, seemed to be borrowing an evolutionary page from the trunked beasts. Giant stag moose with enormous, long-beamed and many-tined antlers alongside caribou and wild sheep—all these inhabited the land bridge during the Ice Age. Meanwhile, stalking the hoofed creatures on padded feet were the fiercest predators this side of the Jurassic: heavily muscled saber-toothed cats with serrated, six-inch-long canines capable of slicing through the thick neck skin of a large ungulate; lions larger than those in Africa today; packs of timber wolves; and the giant short-faced bear, bigger and more menacing than an Alaskan grizzly.

This sketchy picture represented about all that was known about the Bering Land Bridge and the conditions that created it when an unusual woman took an unusual child for a walk in the woods one spring in rural southern New Hampshire.

# Hebe's son

With a conflicting mixture of pride and Yankee reserve, longtime residents of the Monadnock region of southern New Hampshire refer to Greenfield as one of the "younger" villages thereabouts. After all, they say, it wasn't incorporated until 1791. Any local Indians had vanished into the forest before 1770 when settlers began felling trees, clearing land, and putting up log cabins. Between the rocks and stumps, the settlers planted rye, potatoes, and turnips, later adding corn, pumpkins, and beans. They turned loose their pigs to forage in the woods and shot turkeys and other game birds. By 1795, the townsfolk had erected a handsome meetinghouse, joined in 1885 by a two-story schoolhouse, complete with bell tower. In anticipation of the arrival of the railroad, Charles Hopkins built and ran a general store in 1873, later operated by his sons, Walter and Edwin.

Eventually, Edwin's son Donald and Walter's son Charles took over the store and a grain mill they called Granite State Feeds. Donald had started Bates College in Lewiston, Maine, as a premedical student, but ended it as an animal nutrition specialist. There was an art to mixing chicken and cattle and horse feed, reformulating each feed every week so as to use ingredients whose prices were currently low, and still arriving at the guaranteed nutritional analysis. Donald Hopkins had the

A 1974 view of the general store in Greenfield, New Hampshire, built by Hopkins' great-grandfather in 1873 *(Photo by Dave Hopkins, courtesy of Dana Hopkins)*

gift for it, and even wrote papers on the subject for scientific journals. He could identify the sex of chicks too (a trick even the chicken farmers had trouble with) and diagnose diseases and recommend treatments. Donald was short, but lifting hundred-pound grain sacks had made him strong. He was sociable. He loved to sing and play the piano, even the tough Gershwin pieces. Everyone liked him, especially a co-ed at Bates named Henrietta Moody.

On December 26, 1921, a century and a half after the settlers struck their first ax blow in the forests around Greenfield, the young town's youngest resident was David Moody Hopkins, the newborn son of Donald and Henrietta Hopkins. The family's first home was a spacious apartment above the store built by the boy's great-grandfather. The old building was

Donald Hopkins, Dave's father, Greenfield, New Hampshire
*(Photo by Dave Hopkins, courtesy of Dana Hopkins)*

a handsome three-story affair, counting the mansard roof. The front featured a four-columned, frilly trimmed, covered porch off the first two stories. Along one side ran an attached grain shed with three bays into which horse-drawn wagons could be backed for loading. The store sat proudly at the intersection of Greenfield's five principal roads, in the respectable company of the church, the school, and the library. Along these roads were about sixty wood frame houses. Behind the houses were fields. Behind the fields, woods.

Henrietta loved the woods. She had grown up on a farm down east in Turner, Maine, where she was particularly close to a maiden aunt, as she would have been described in those days. Aunt Nell, according to family lore, could name every wildflower found in forest or field in that part of Maine, and during many long walks, she passed on this knowledge to her admiring protégé. Though she never married and had no children, Aunt Nell left spiritual progeny. With those walks, she established a family tradition that has continued now for five generations, about one hundred years.

"Henry" to her own kin, Henrietta was Hebe (Hee-bee) to the Hopkins side of the family and to her friends in Greenfield. "Hebe" was not a standard diminutive, not a childhood mispronunciation, but survived from her college days, the result of Donald's familiarity with Greek and Roman mythology. Donald and Henrietta sometimes participated in weekend house parties. At these events, which were common then among college students, a group would rent a cottage on a lake. Everyone would swim, cook meals, and divide the chores. When Henrietta drew the chore of emptying the chamber pot, Donald christened her Hebe, after a nymph in Greek mythology dubbed "cup bearer to the gods." She bore it (the name, that is) for the rest of her life.

Henrietta Moody, Hopkins' mother, as a girl in 1914
*(Photo courtesy of Dana Hopkins)*

With the appearance of Dave's younger sister, Dona, the family outgrew the apartment and moved a few hundred yards away to a fine old two-story wood frame house on Forest Road built by Dave's great-grand uncle in 1874. Another baby, Dan, came along, and in the evenings, when Donald's work day was done, he read books like *Black Beauty* to the children. For her part, Hebe could hardly wait until her first born was old enough to be taken into the woods and shown the plants and animals, just as her Aunt Nell had done for her. That day finally came in late May when Dave was five years old, and he still remembers the flowers she introduced to him on that first walk: "She showed me a ground nut, which was a spring flower with a little raisin-sized bulb under it. She showed me star flowers, which are little white flowers with five rays like a star. She showed me sweet fern, which is not really a fern and has little seeds the size of wheat grains that you can eat. She showed me Jack-in-the-pulpit. She showed me trilliums with their triple leaves and triple blossoms. And on down into the swampy woods where there were lady slippers." Hebe would sometimes pile up a little brush around the lady slippers to protect them from flower pickers.

Dave's walks with his mother continued until she decided that the town was small enough and he was big enough that he could be left to explore the woods alone. She had shown him the trails and paths so he could find his way home again. From then on, with a bang of the screen door, Dave was out of the house, over the stone wall, across the field, and into Gypson's Woods. There were "hills, mountains, swamps, lakes and ponds, brooks and rivers, and nearly all of it was forested." He loved the woods because of all that was there. But he also loved it as a sort of escape habitat: It offered relief from his mother, who was strict. She both led him into the woods, he

Henrietta Moody Hopkins (Hebe) and Dave, undated
*(Courtesy of Dana Hopkins)*

laughs, and drove him into it. "She set me free for years and years of explorations."

These forays were mostly, but not always solitary. And, more often than not, when Dave and his pals addressed themselves to the lower vertebrate fauna of Gypson's Woods, it was with an eye toward inflating a frog. They would insert the hollow stem cut from the bamboolike *Equisetum* plant into a frog's rectum and blow. As the superbuoyant frog struggled in vain to dive to the bottom, the boys would collapse in paroxysms of hysterical laughter.

But Dave's interests went further. Gypson's Woods was his refuge and he its warden. And there was a lot that needed to be done. The more accessible critters, particularly, needed to be rounded up and brought home for further study. He found where the amphibians laid their eggs and scooped them up in his bucket. Toads' eggs looked like strings of pearls attached to semisubmerged grass stems in shallow water. The salamander's eggs were a compact mass, he noticed, while frog eggs were "kind of more bumpy." He discovered that the wood tortoises laid their eggs in the warmth of the south-facing railroad embankment near Granite State Feeds, the Hopkins' family mill. Land-loving and about ten inches across, the tortoises were easy to catch. Dave had about a dozen of them in a half-buried washtub filled with water and rocks. Also in residence were a few garter snakes and salamanders. Some of these specimens he kept in the crate that brought the family's first electric refrigerator. When his friend and mentor, George Proctor, the actual game warden, showed up with a huge snapping turtle, Dave was both delighted and terrified. It was about three feet across and, like most of its breed, aggressive. Proctor had taken it from a fish trap, probably to spare the trout. All of these things Dave cared for or tried to hatch in the pots and

View across fields and stone walls to Gypson's Woods, opposite Hopkins' home in Greenfield, New Hampshire
*(Photo by Dan O'Neill)*

pans, tubs, and gallon-sized mayonnaise jars that crowded his base of herpetological investigations, the carriage shed.

Worms, too, were of interest. Out behind the mill sat a great mound of chaff, blown there from the screens in the oat mill. The chaff mound was slightly damp and actively fermenting, so it was warm below the surface, an ideal snake egg incubator. Probing for snake eggs one day, Dave dug into a thriving colony of small red worms. They were about an inch and a half long and very wiggly. Soon he had several regular clients. Dr. Keyes, the dentist, happily paid for worms, as did the Reverend Mr. Weston, the Unitarian preacher in nearby Hancock. It was no problem at all for Dave to dig and sell two hundred worms on order to the town's fishermen heading out to Sunset Lake.

Hopkins (front row, third from left) with his first grade class, c. 1926 *(Courtesy of Dana Hopkins)*

When he acquired hip boots, Dave started stalking the swampy margins of ephemeral ponds, especially on spring nights when the peepers were singing or on midsummer nights when the bullfrogs croaked from the larger lakes. As he crept forward, the frogs would stop their chorus all at once, as if on the baton stroke of a hidden conductor. Once in position, he would stand very still, his finger on the button of his flashlight. Eventually the frogs' wariness would yield to an overpowering urge to mate, and they'd start croaking again. Straining his powers of auditory location, Dave would take aim and shoot out his beam. The prize: catching one with its throat popped out.

Throughout this period, Dave had only a vague idea of what a scientist was. In his mind, two things defined the profession: a white lab coat and a microscope. These were to a scientist what a leather vest and a six-shooter were to a cowboy, he thought. On the whole, the prospect of riding the range of a laboratory and drawing down on germs with a microscope did not present a powerfully romantic image. But a *naturalist*, that was something else. A naturalist tramped through swamps and jungles. He collected frogs, snakes, and bugs. Roy Ditmars was a naturalist. The great herpetologist (reptile and amphibian specialist) worked at the American Museum of Natural History in New York. Dave had read his books and pictured him as a sort of hard-eyed Randolph Scott with a bush hat and a python draped across his shoulders. "I could relate to that!" he says.

Pretty soon, Dave was pressing plants and collecting their seeds in packets. Along with his diary, he kept a scientific journal in which, among other things, he speculated about the life cycle of newts. They hatched as very small pollywogs with frilly external gills. Later they grew legs and looked like aquatic salamanders. Then they seemed to emerge from the ponds as the familiar red newts with vertical slots where the gills had been. Still later, they metamorphosed again, turned green, and returned to a life in the nearby lakes and ponds. There wasn't a great deal of literature on these faunas. No one was collecting or publishing field guides. But what literature did exist—like Roy Ditmars' work—Dave got hold of, usually from a larger library in a neighboring village. It is likely that by the time he finished high school, Dave knew as much about the lower vertebrate fauna in his part of southern New Hampshire as anyone alive.

Hebe took her son on other types of walks, too. She lived at a time when middle-class women, even college-trained ones like herself, generally did not work outside the home. And though she was usually on the school board and often on church committees, these things did not exhaust either her energy or her intellectual capacities. With two women friends her age, Florence Adams and Ruth Ledward, she set out to write a history of Greenfield, population 396. They reviewed written sources, government documents, and maps. But they also interviewed the old farmers and their wives about the things they could remember and the things they had heard from their parents. "In their cow-smelling parlors, they told my mother about old stage coach inns, about old murders. They didn't have that name for it," he says, "but they were collecting 'oral history.'"

Hebe and Dave heard the account of Daniel Kimball who, while he cleared his land off Mountain Road in the late 1700s, slept in a hollow log, stopping the opening with a stump to keep out prowling animals. Another tale that survived from 1831 told of a man who was murdered that year, apparently for the proceeds of the sale of his oxen. He was thought to have been set upon at Roger's Corner and buried somewhere in the embankment of Forest Road, then under construction. One legend had it that a townsman received a very comely yoke of oxen in trade for his wife. She was probably not Molly Whittemore, who, as Hebe recorded, decided that her husband was unsuitably clothed on the eve of his departure for the Revolutionary War, so she "sheared a black sheep, prepared the wool, spun the yarn, wove the cloth, and cut and made a pair of pantaloons; all this, supposedly, within twenty-four hours!"

Besides this lore, Hebe and her collaborators assembled the history of a century and a half of settlement, industry, and civic works. She built a dossier on each house in Greenfield. On maps, she plotted the names of the forgotten farmers, the locations of their vanished farmsteads and of the long gone roads that connected them. With these notes in hand, Hebe and her friends, frequently with Dave in tow, took to the woods and fields to ground-truth the information. For her, it was intellectual exercise and just plain exercise. For Dave, it was training in the methodologies of science and history, though at the time he knew it only as fun.

Because Greenfield is in a formerly glaciated area, the soil is thin (most of it having been bulldozed by the glacier into southern Massachusetts and Connecticut). Because the soil is thin, ledges of rock poke through. And because rocks littered the fields, farmers had to clear the stones. One method was to drop them next to a boulder too big to move, until the assemblage looked like a lithified hen and a clutch of stony eggs. But the usual technique was to haul the rocks to the margin of the field in a stone boat and build a wall there, sometimes on either side of a roadway. Thus, long after the glacier had melted, it continued, indirectly, to influence the placement of rock on the surface of the land. When Hebe and Dave went out to find an old road overgrown for a hundred years, it was often a parallel pair of stone walls they found. Once conspicuous at the edge of hayfields and cornfields and pastures—a gridwork delimiting the township—the walls now crept, tumbled down and covered with bracken, through the shadowy understory of a pine forest.

One such road fossil that Hebe found was to the northeast of the village. As she wrote in *A Brief History of Greenfield, New Hampshire, 1791–1941*, coauthored with Ruth Ledward, the road was "discernible only by the two stone walls marching sturdily up hill and down, across brooks and through thick underbrush." Dave and Hebe kept an eye out for what he called "the shadow marks left on the land by nine or ten generations of Yankee farmers and settlers," finding depressions that might mark foundations or cellar holes. Likewise, they looked for lilacs or *Spirea*, probable relics of a former farmyard, or crabapple trees, once productive trees that became too shaded and untended. They found "pocks and pits in boulders and ledges where, my mother told me, Indians had ground acorns." And on the leaf-strewn bottom of Whittemore Pond they could just make out a submerged dugout canoe, possibly made by Indians.

Working this way, like an archeologist, Hebe located the house site of Isaac Butterfield, who had been a major in the Continental Army:

> He lived on a road, now abandoned. ... A depression marks the site of the home he built. His door stone with his initials and date, I.B. 1779, crudely carved, may be seen nearby. This stone, with the inscription outward, at a later date was put into the wall bordering the road and was familiar to the many who passed that way. More recently the stone has fallen backward out of the wall, face up, and would now be unnoticed unless the dead leaves were brushed away from the inscription.

On the lawn in front of an old brick house, Hebe found the all but hidden traces of Amos Whittemore's 1770 log cabin, one of the first structures built in Greenfield. "When there is a sprinkling of snow on the ground, the very slight depressions marking the outlines of the cabin may still be seen," she wrote. And taking all this in was a young boy fascinated with both the fact and the techniques of uncovering the past.

With a late December birthday, Dave was the youngest in his class when he entered first grade. The school had two teachers: one for grades one through four, the other for grades five through eight. Dave always had his nose in a book. He would even read as he walked down the street to the store or the post office or to Mrs. Gage's house, where he did chores for a small allowance. "Once he was so preoccupied with reading he walked into a telephone pole," says his brother Dan. "And a neighbor who observed the incident, out of concern, called my mother to tell her about it." But Dave did so well in school that after the seventh grade he was sent right on to Peterborough High School, seven miles away. It was a good school. Small, with fewer than two hundred enrolled, the students had the same teachers from year to year. Lively young Iyla Tracy, his English teacher, recognized Dave's talent as a writer and occasionally took him and two or three other students into Boston to see a play. Once, they learned a whole play in French and read it at an experimental television station in Boston. And there was his favorite teacher, Flossy (not to her face) Hancock, who taught Dave math for four years. Using a map of the Peterborough quadrangle, she had the class cut out cardboard along the contours and build up a relief map. As a trigonometry lesson, she took the students outside to survey the school grounds with transit and rod. During spring vacation, when they were seniors and old enough to drive, Dave and his best friend drove up to visit her at her family's home near Dixville Notch.

Less pleasant was typing class. From his first encounter with Miss S——, it was a case of instant and mutual dislike. He thought her "shaped like one of those darning balls you stick in socks." She seemed to disapprove of Dave's very existence. He could type like a tornado, but Miss S——, also known as The Hawk, saw only the errors. To make matters worse, she presided over his study hall as well, so that each day held two periods of misery for both of them. Dave ended up cutting school quite a lot, and Miss S—— would call his father at the mill to ask if he knew that Dave was not in school.

Oddly enough, Miss S—— also taught a class in earth science called physiography. It concerned the origin and shaping of landscape features (a study now subsumed by what is called geomorphology). Copies of Isaiah Bowman's *Forest Physiography* were scattered around her classroom, and inevitably Dave picked one up. The book had been published in 1911, a time when descriptive studies of the landscape were sometimes the province of geology, sometimes of geography. Bowman happened to be a geographer, but one with an interest in natural history and geomorphology. To Dave, the book's blending of disciplines seemed almost designed to seize his interest. He had already become aware, through one particular walk with his mother, of processes that shape the landscape. She was one of the few people who knew the location, deep in the woods, of the Great Gulf, a tree-choked, rocky gorge that cut through the shoulder of North Pack Monadnock Mountain. When the glaciers that covered New Hampshire began to melt at the end of the last Ice Age, rising water collected in an impoundment behind a ridge between Crotched Mountain and North Pack Monadnock Mountain north of Greenfield. Eventually, it breached the ridge, and meltwater roared through in a tremendous cataract as it cut first a notch, then a canyon three or four miles long. Dave followed his mother as she scrambled down into the "very mysterious, almost frightening" gorge, where he delighted in the beech grove that filled it. He thought beech forests especially beautiful, because they typically lack underbrush or litter. Walking among the white trunks he imagined himself in his own secret park. But he was even more enthralled with the rocky cliffs of the gorge itself. He remembers thinking, "Hey, we can really see what the glacier did here." It was physiography in the flesh.

If The Hawk noticed the boy's growing passion for geology, she did not encourage it to the extent of suggesting he take her courses. Today Dave says it's funny that he couldn't see the obvious: Physiography was an unusual course; it didn't fit in with anything else in the curriculum; clearly, it was only offered because of Miss S——'s own keen interest in the subject. He regrets that while the two shared a special interest, it was riven by a chasm of mutual disapproval. Still, Miss S—— influenced Dave (through a process something like magnetic repulsion) toward a book and thus to a science that would become his life's work. The precocious boy, a natural-born natural historian who should have been Miss S——'s star pupil and who launched a brilliant career in her room, never took her course. Except typing, in which he salvaged a D.

With an education like this, beginning with his first walk in the woods, it is not surprising that Hebe's son would spend most of his life searching for clues of ancient landscapes. For, while the country around Greenfield was laced with the vestiges of extinct byways and pocked with all but obscured depressions that had once been houses, so too was Beringia. And Dave Hopkins would draw on natural history, oral history, archeology, and geology to piece together the story of the greatest ancient thoroughfare of all: the Bering Land Bridge.

# 4
# CALLING

Dave was obsessed with trains. From the age of seven, he spent his Saturdays hanging around the railroad tracks in Greenfield, waiting for the noon freight. At the station, he'd pass the time with Frank Gage, the Boston & Maine station agent whom he worshipped. Dave loved smelling the smoke of his Edgeworth tobacco as the telegraph clicked and the flies buzzed. He loved listening to Mr. Gage's stories about his big trip out west in the 1880s, when he was a car tracer for the Old Colony Railroad. And always Mr. Gage would wind up by saying, "Well, David, one of these days when Old Amos is on, I'm going to get you a ride on that engine."

About that, Dave had decidedly mixed feelings. Somehow, it was both the thing he wanted most in the world to do, and the thing he was most terrified of—thinking he would either die outright or that his father would murder him. But one day when Dave was on the freight house platform watching the train crew wheel freight out of the way car with hand trucks, and just when he thought Mr. Gage was safely up at the station, he suddenly felt a firm hand on his shoulder. "Well, David, you're in luck. Old Amos is on today."

He remembers that first ride clearly. They chugged down to the mill where his father worked. Old Amos pulled the levers, and the fireman, Merton Smith, himself fifty-five, shoveled

Locomotive beside Granite State Feeds, the Hopkins family grain mill in Greenfield, New Hampshire, where Dave worked for forty cents an hour *(Photo by Dave Hopkins, courtesy of Dana Hopkins)*

coal. The mill hands all saw Dave and waved. He waved back, gulping. To bring the cars out of the mill, the engine went in, grabbed them using a coupler in front of the cowcatcher, and backed out. To get the cars back behind the engine where they belonged, the engineer did a flying switch. "They had a string of perhaps three boxcars. The brakeman would be riding out on the pilot, or cowcatcher, and another brakeman would be standing by the switch that led into the passing track. So, they would start accelerating, backing up, and when they got going real good, the brakeman up front would pull the pin cutting loose the boxcars. The engine would be CH-CH-CH-CH-CH-CH-CH-CH, charging up the track as fast as it could go in order to get away from the cars. The boxcars would drift along behind, and as the engine passed the siding; the other brakeman would throw the switch, sending boxcars onto the sidetrack. Then we would be able to move down, back up, and pick them up. That maneuver never stopped exciting me. It's dangerous, and it's also illegal."

While on the locomotive, he had been blowing the whistle, ringing bells, poking into the firebox, just "having one absolute hell of a time," he says. To his amazement, Dave found that his father didn't mind at all. From then on, he was up on the locomotive moving freight every Saturday. And when Merton Smith started firing on the passenger train, Dave would ride with him up to Elmwood and go fishing in the mill pond during the three-hour layover before returning to Greenfield and points east. Once he even accompanied Mr. Smith all the way to Nashua, Lowell, and Boston. At each place, they went into the roundhouse and Dave climbed all over the gigantic engines.

By the time he entered the University of New Hampshire, Dave Hopkins knew two things. First, he knew that his true calling in life was to be a railroad brakeman. Second, he knew that his folks wouldn't stand for it. So he enrolled in the engineering program, thinking he might work designing freight cars. "All of this sounds strange," says Hopkins today, "but nonetheless that's the way my mind was working." He found, however, that engineering involved aptitudes he lacked. He was drawn to biology, geology, psychology, and creative writing. And socialism. As a kid, Dave was keenly aware of economic injustices during the Great Depression. He saw hobos and tramps knock at his backdoor asking for food from his family, which was clearly prospering. Inchoate feelings of shame—or at least civic responsibility—began to form themselves into a liberal, socialistic, and public service–oriented philosophy that would guide him for the rest of his life. Less encumbered by these sensibilities, some of the workers at the mill back home, on learning of Dave's leftist political leanings, took to calling him New Hampshire Red, an epithet all the more cutting because that was also the name of a new breed of New Hampshire chicken. Eventually, after letting his intellectual interests roam a bit, he settled on geology.

In the summer of 1942 Dave enrolled at Harvard as a doctoral student. But he hadn't been there three weeks when a telegram arrived asking if he would accept employment with the U.S. Geological Survey in Alaska. In those days the USGS recruited from the Civil Service exam, and most students took the test in their senior year. Dave had done pretty well, and in the early 1940s the USGS was expanding rapidly to locate strategic minerals for the war effort. The war at once presented an opportunity to move forward and a disincentive to stand still: As a twenty-year-old student, Dave was draft bait.

Hopkins as an undergraduate at the University of New Hampshire on a geology field trip *(Clipping from* The Boston Globe, *undated, courtesy of Dave Hopkins)*

His advisors at Harvard encouraged him to take the job now and finish school later—just the advice he was hoping to hear. He wired his acceptance to the Survey, rushed home to New Hampshire, packed some things, and headed out to Seattle.

The expansion had been so sudden that the Survey was pressed to find an experienced person to manage all the logistics of enrolling the new employees mustering in Seattle and outfitting them for a summer in Alaska. The most experienced person they could come up with was Hopkins' best friend Clyde Wharhaftig. "Clyde was a very nervous person, very conscientious and dedicated—and a terrible administrator. So there was Clyde having to meet all these guys at the train, find them hotels, take them to Filson to buy tin pants [made of paraffin-soaked canvas], tin coats and shoe pacs [rubber-bottomed boots with thick felt liners], get tents purchased, get us sworn in, and finally put us on Alaska Steam ships and point us off toward Alaska. ... Clyde made several mistakes—one of them was that he sent Ethelbert Unklesbay to Seward Peninsula when he was supposed to go to the town of Seward on the Kenai Peninsula, about 1,500 steamer miles away." For those traveling by train once in Alaska, Wharhaftig reminded them they were each entitled to first class accommodations and a Pullman berth and to be sure to insist upon it. "You probably know," says Hopkins, "there were not then, and there never have been any Pullmans on the Alaska Railroad."

Another of Wharhaftig's missteps had been to pair Jack Kingston and Don Miller on an expedition to join a senior geologist named Moffet in Alaska's Copper River country. Not a good match, says Hopkins. "Kingston was extremely loquacious, and Miller was so silent that one could be with him for an hour and only have three or four words from him. So

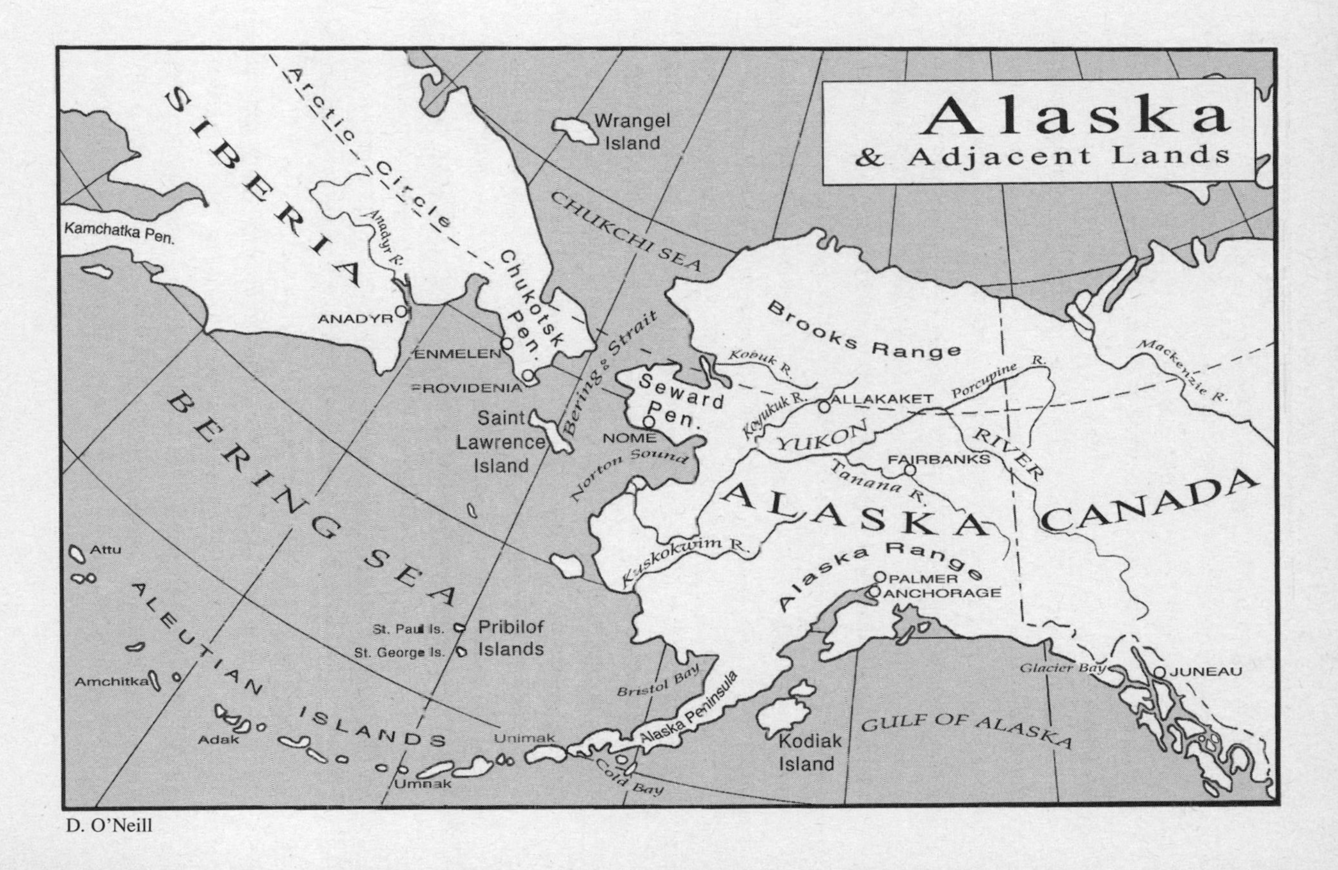

Alaska
& Adjacent Lands
SIBERIA
Arctic Circle
Anadyr R.
Kamchatka Pen.
ANADYR
Wrangel Island
CHUKCHI SEA
Chukotsk Pen.
ENMELEN
PROVIDENIA
Bering Strait
Saint Lawrence Island
Seward Pen.
NOME
Norton Sound
Brooks Range
Kobuk R.
Koyukuk R.
ALLAKAKET
Porcupine R.
Mackenzie R.
YUKON
RIVER
FAIRBANKS
Tanana R.
ALASKA
CANADA
Kuskokwim R.
Alaska Range
PALMER
ANCHORAGE
Glacier Bay
JUNEAU
BERING SEA
Attu
ALEUTIAN ISLANDS
St. Paul Is.
St. George Is.
Pribilof Islands
Amchitka
Adak
Unimak
Umnak
Bristol Bay
Alaska Peninsula
Cold Bay
Kodiak Island
GULF OF ALASKA
D. O'Neill

they had a long backpacking journey to join Moffet. It was torture for both of them—Jack talking all the way, and Miller grunting because he got tired of saying 'yes.'"

After some weeks in Seattle, Hopkins was sworn in as, he says, the Survey's "youngest and least well-trained geologist at the age of twenty." He sailed up the Inside Passage in Southeast Alaska to Juneau, where he had a week to kill before he could hire a boat out to the field camp. "So I got drunk every night and hung around these low bars where I got to know the whores. I just have vignettes—little snapshot memories of that period. One of them is four o'clock in the morning in a back room behind a bar with a bunch of low types in one of these structures that are built on stilts out over the water. I feel I was really lucky to experience this ancient residue of the gold rush in Juneau."

Finally, on a clear summer day, he boarded a boat that chugged out into Icy Strait, where humpback whales leaped, rolled in midair, and crashed down with tremendous splashes. In Glacier Bay National Park, Hopkins thrilled to see sparkling white icebergs dotting the emerald green fjords, and massive glaciers coursing down from snowy peaks ten thousand feet high to terminate at saltwater in icy blue walls. Hopkins found the USGS camp on a small mountain half surrounded by glaciers on Muir Inlet. That night, he crawled into his tent under a clear, still-bright sky and slept to the rumble of distant thunder.

The next morning, with the sky still cloudless, he realized the rumbling hadn't come from the collision of clouds of vaporized water, but from the collision of masses of solid and liquid water, as skyscraper-sized pinnacles of ice cracked off the floating face of Muir Glacier and boomed down into the bay below. Hopkins had studied glaciers in college. The University of New Hampshire even sat on an ancient glacial deposit. But he had never seen anything like this: monstrous, active, live glaciers shouldering their way into his consciousness, day and night. When he wasn't hiking up on the glaciers, or exploring the blue ice caves beneath them, or running the skiff out to the bigger bergs that floated by like crystalline islands, he just filled his eyes with the sight of these relics of the Ice Age. In between time, he helped to map a molybdenum deposit, a strategic mineral.

The next summer, 1943, Hopkins returned to Alaska, looking for coal deposits in the mountain-rimmed Matanuska Valley. He loved the summers of fieldwork not only because it gave him the chance to explore nature in a wild and beautiful country, but also because fieldwork in Alaska was a seat-of-the-pants proposition, unpredictable and varied. In those days, he says, an Alaskan geologist was a generalist, "measuring the dips and strikes in Birch Creek Schist today, mapping glacial moraines tomorrow, collecting bones in the Pleistocene muck the day after that." Each fall, though, he had to head back to the Survey's offices in Washington, D.C., which he liked much less well. To make the best of it, he made the trip east on one or another of the famous transcontinental railroad routes like the Great Northern's Empire Builder and the Milwaukee's Olympian. But by the summer of 1944, Uncle Sam's bony finger was tracking his movements. Hoping that being drafted in Alaska would mean a posting there, Hopkins lingered on into the fall, writing up his summer's work. The tap on the shoulder came shortly, and he was inducted at Ft. Richardson near Anchorage on December 7, 1944, the third anniversary of Pearl Harbor.

At the end of basic training, when it came time to give the new recruits assignments, the Army administered intelligence and aptitude tests. They also queried each soldier as to his education, training, and experience and whether there was any sort of specialized work that he felt suited for. Without hesitation, Hopkins declared himself best utilized as a brakeman in the railroad battalion of the Alaska Railroad. On the questionnaire, he declared that he had been a brakeman on the Lincoln & East Branch Railroad. It was a nice little logging road that poked up into the canyons of the White Mountains in northern New Hampshire. More to the point, it was so obscure that he figured the Army would never be able to check up on his fabricated employment there. As a second choice, he mentioned his experience as a geologist searching for coal to power the military bases and the railroad. It was just possible that this might lead to a reassignment to the USGS. And finally, in an anything-but-the-infantry fallback strategy, he claimed that he was a trained weather observer. He had, in fact, completed a class in climatology, and on a few occasions had watched his friend Art Fernald take the weather observations on the roof of the geology building at the University of New Hampshire.

The Army took one look at Hopkins' weatherman experience and sent him to the storm kitchen of the hemisphere: Cold Bay, Alaska. Six hundred fifty miles west of Anchorage, at the base of the Aleutian Chain, Cold Bay sits between the stormy waters of the North Pacific and those of the Bering Sea. Still, Hopkins had a lot of fun there. On crisp, clear mornings, the symmetrical, white cone of seven-thousand-foot Mount Pavlof, forty miles to the east, might be gray-tipped with fresh volcanic ash. Pavlof was almost always smoking, and more than once produced smoke rings rising through the dawn sky.

He launched instrumented weather balloons, recorded temperatures, and plotted the wind speed and direction at various altitudes with radar. In his free time, which was most of the time, he packed Eric Hultén's *Flora of the Aleutian Islands* up onto the treeless flanks of Frosty Peak, where he collected plants. Many years later, his mother sent this collection of Aleutian plants to the Smithsonian Institution, which was very glad to have it.

If all this botanical work suggests Hopkins was ambivalent about geology, he was. Geologically unexplored, Cold Bay presented a tremendous opportunity for a professional to do original mapping. But it was an opportunity Hopkins did not seize. Notwithstanding his couple of years' employment at USGS, he was not at all sure if he was drawn more to geology than to natural history, generally. He wasn't even sure he wanted to do graduate work in any subject. "I felt swept along without exercise of my will," he says. "This is really loony, but I thought my father and I could raise chickens in the Matanuska Valley. In the first place, I hate chickens. I had to raise them in 4-H. I hate the smell of chicken shit." But Hopkins was recalling with some nostalgia the family mill, the rich smells of the air laden with grain dust, and the din of great belts whirling in every direction.

Before he could ponder further his prospects in poultry, Hopkins' army career ended explosively. One spring day in 1946, after the war had ended, while he was standing at the teletype in Cold Bay, the machine began clattering wildly. Reports were coming in of a volcanic eruption in Okmok Caldera on Umnak Island, a couple hundred miles farther out along the Aleutians. The collapsed volcanic edifice, once eight or ten thousand feet high, was spewing fine ash onto nearby

Fort Glenn and potentially damaging the engines of the DC-3s and P-38s that patrolled along The Chain. It took a full-blown eruption to awaken the Army to the fact that its Aleutian air bases were sitting on the flanks of active volcanoes. Hopkins was given an early discharge, assigned to the USGS, and sent to Umnak Island to work on an army-funded study of Alaska volcanoes. With the war over, the Umnak assignment lasted only a few months, and Hopkins joined the stream of young men taking up the GI Bill and heading back to school.

At Harvard's geology department, Kirk Bryan was a brilliant maverick, and Hopkins quickly fell under his influence. He "lavishly bestowed on his students instructions on how to think, how to work and how to live," says Hopkins. Unlike traditional geologists, Bryan approached problems by looking for leads within several disciplines. He was prepared, for example, to look at such things as fossil pollen to see what it might reveal about ancient climates. Knowledge of the climate history might delineate episodes of glaciation. That, in turn, might help explain the shape of the present landscape. "In Kirk Bryan, I found a geologist interested in *geoarcheology*, which hadn't even been invented yet! Here was a geologist interested in the new subject of permafrost and frost action." Under Bryan, Hopkins began to see himself as a paleonaturalist, blending his childhood interests in a range of natural history subjects with the geologic history of the landscape. "Although he presented himself to us as an expert on practically everything, he was an extremely subversive man, constantly teaching us to question all authority and all authorities. But the most important thing I learned from him was to give a good idea its head." Hopkins' catholic inclinations coalesced as an interdisciplinary approach to scientific research. His attraction to the earth's most recent geologic history resulted in his earning one of Harvard's first Ph.D. degrees in Quaternary geology, the period spanning the last two million years and characterized by the Ice Ages. Through his employment at the USGS, Hopkins' interests became focused on Alaska; and when shortly he came up with a good idea concerning the Bering Land Bridge, he gave it its head.

# 5

# FIELDWORK IN ARCTIC ALASKA

On a sunny evening in the summer of 1948, on the east shore of a small lake eighty-four miles northeast of Nome, Alaska, four men and a dog sat on the ground in the lee of a white canvas wall tent. Nearby, a fifth man busied himself skinning a rodent. The four men played bridge but, like the dog, were alert for any sound indicating the near availability of food. The fifth man, Bill Quay, the camp cook, went about his business unhurriedly, more intent on peeling the skins from voles and lemmings than from potatoes and carrots. Quay was a mammalogy student. He dug pit traps around the camp and collected small mammals: shrews, lemmings, voles, and an occasional ground squirrel. These he skinned and prepared as study specimens. He was usually still at this task when twenty-six-year-old Dave Hopkins and his USGS field crew tromped into camp in the early evening, exhausted and ravenous. For a couple of hours, while they waited on dinner, the men played bridge and voiced their suspicions as to the probable rodent content of the stew in progress. When it finally arrived, they were grateful for chunks of meat and fat, whatever their origin.

After sitting nearly idle in Nome for the better part of June, Hopkins could write home on the thirtieth that he had finally

Tents in a big wind at Lava Lake, July 4, 1948
*(Photo by Dave Hopkins, courtesy of Dana Hopkins)*

been able to get an Army PBY floatplane to haul the field crew to Lava Lake and was "in the field at last." Wading ashore with their gear, the crew found a cache of old oil drums, canvas, tent poles, and wooden boxes—remnants of an earlier encampment of a small detachment of Army weathermen. They set up an eight-by-ten wall tent for the kitchen, and pitched two more eight-by-eight tents for sleeping quarters. As a cache for the grub, they arranged the oil drums into four walls and roofed them with boards and canvas. Where a little creek flowed toward the lake, Quay built a dam and rigged up a stove pipe flume leading to a big washtub, thus providing running water to the middle of camp. Ingenuity was at work at the other end of the water cycle, as well. The deluxe latrine featured, over the customary hole in the ground, the upper portion of a pot-bellied stove with the lid removed. A superstructure of two-by-fours supported walls of mosquito netting, but "the resulting cage," Hopkins wrote, "was an atrium for a thousand mosquitoes, rather than a sanctuary for humans."

A pair of muskrats lived near camp and liked to climb up and wash themselves on a dock built of oil drums and planks. But the most bountiful wildlife was the nesting migratory birds. "Whenever I sit down to take notes," Hopkins wrote home, "I am surrounded with chipping and chirping birds appearing from every bush and tussock." He noted tiny redpolls and white-capped sparrows, longspurs with their black throats and rusty collars, yellow wagtails, tawny willow thrushes and some kind of warbler. "Every patch of brush," he wrote, "is noisy with the fluttering of wings." The lake drew in

Sigafoos, Hopkins, and Fernald building the meat cache at Lava Lake, 1948 *(Courtesy of Dana Hopkins)*

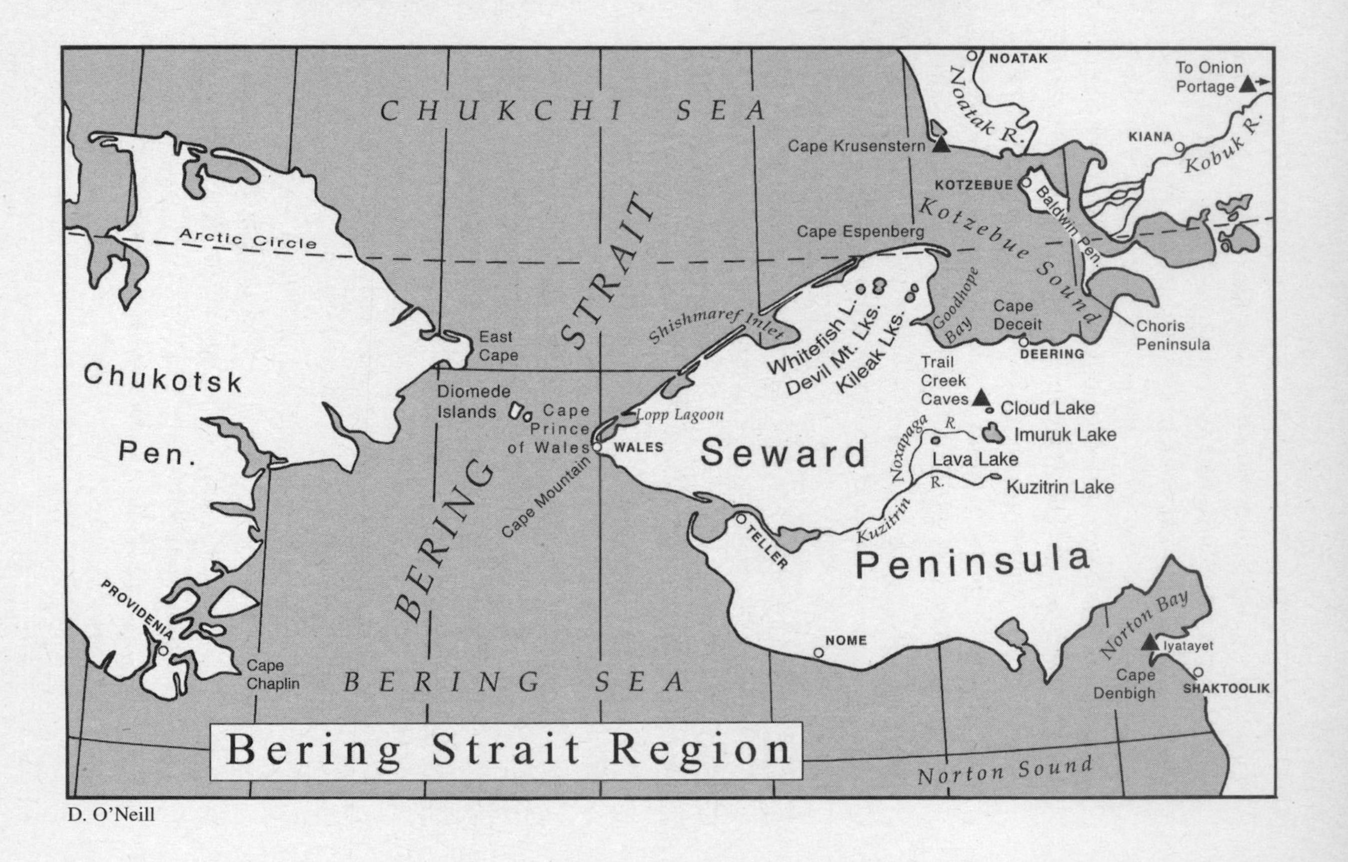

CHUKCHI SEA
NOATAK
Noatak R.
To Onion Portage
KIANA
Kobuk R.
Cape Krusenstern
KOTZEBUE
Baldwin Pen.
Kotzebue Sound
Arctic Circle
Cape Espenberg
STRAIT
Shishmaref Inlet
Whitefish L.
Devil Mt. Lks.
Kileak Lks.
Goodhope Bay
Cape Deceit
DEERING
Choris Peninsula
East Cape
Chukotsk Pen.
Trail Creek Caves
Cloud Lake
Diomede Islands
Cape Prince of Wales
Lopp Lagoon
WALES
Seward Peninsula
Noxapaga R.
Imuruk Lake
Lava Lake
Kuzitrin R.
Kuzitrin Lake
BERING
Cape Mountain
TELLER
PROVIDENIA
NOME
Norton Bay
Iyatayet
Cape Chaplin
BERING SEA
Cape Denbigh
SHAKTOOLIK
Bering Strait Region
Norton Sound
D. O'Neill

waterfowl too: oldsquaws, eiders, scoters, scaups, and loons. "I'm seeing swans daily—they're graceful flyers and the first thing I notice is the sound of wings and a very high soprano croak, and then I see them drop into some nearby lake." Canada geese gathered in noisy conventions on the Noxapaga River just west of the lake. Ptarmigan and snipe inhabited the uplands; while marauding jaegers patrolled overhead, always ready to destroy a nest of eggs or pick off a young bird. Higher still, in the outermost orbits of the winged world, the watchful eagles drifted.

When recruiting crew members for summer fieldwork, Hopkins could be a bit zealous in his quest for diversity. Even the cook had to contribute to his widening interests. One year, when he was leafing through a big stack of Form 57s, the federal government's personnel form, he spotted an interesting cook prospect. Two things caught his eye: The fellow was Iranian-born, and he answered yes to all the questions that asked whether his history contained instances of moral turpitude or affiliation with the Communist party. Hopkins hired him at once, anticipating dinners of spicy kabobs and provocative political conversation. At that summer's field camp,however, he discovered that the fellow's inclinations—both gastronomical and philosophical—were mild to the point of bland. Discreetly, Hopkins probed. It turned out the cook was the son of a missionary, hence the Iranian connection and perhaps the mainstream politics. As for moral turpitude and Communist leanings, he said he'd become impatient filling out the government's long personnel form. After plodding through a series of questions that all called for an affirmative response, he'd simply run down the rest of the list checking all the yes boxes.

Hopkins at Hammum Creek, near Imuruk River, 1948
*(Courtesy of Dana Hopkins)*

For his present crew, Hopkins had assembled a varied bunch. There was Quay, the cook/mammalogist, who, as Hopkins wrote his parents, "spends more time trapping, shooting and skinning animals and birds than he does cooking and taking care of camp, but that suits me fine and suits the rest of the fellows, too." There was Art Fernald and Jim Seitz, both geology graduate students whom Hopkins thought well-trained and capable of working alone. And there was the fellow Hopkins was the most glad to have along, Bob Sigafoos, a big Dutchman from Ohio who was working on a Ph.D. in botany at Harvard. Hopkins had met him in an ecology seminar and found him to be a good talker as well as smart, witty, and thoroughly rebellious about received knowledge. On previous field trips, Hopkins had been collecting plants and trying to identify them on his own. Now he could work alongside a trained botanist. Most days, the two went off together. Each evening Sigafoos would take the lantern into his tent, using it to dry the day's collected plants, then press them between sheets of clean newsprint bought from the *Nome Nugget*. The bridge game always waited on Sigafoos' completion of that chore.

Rounding out the crew was Chuk (short for Inmachuk), a sled dog pup Hopkins had brought along, but who was not universally popular in camp. "The trouble started when a lot of our limited supply of fresh meat—I guess all of it—disappeared from where we had cached it within a day or two of setting up camp. We were reduced to fried Spam. And for a week or more, we would sit in our 8 × 10 cook tent, eating our fried Spam, door open, but mosquito net unfurled. Presently, we became aware of Chuk gnawing on a pork chop, right in front of the tent door. Later, as we'd be cleaning up the dishes, our little yellow dog would stagger into the tent, burping. Jim never forgave the pup, and the others never liked dogs anyway, so he was pretty much my dog thereafter."

The crew's official mission was to investigate a huge area—more than three hundred square miles—of lava flows in the Imuruk Lake region on behalf of the Engineer Intelligence

Wilbur (Bill) Quay and Bob Sigafoos on Skeleton Buttek, Seward Peninsula, 1948 *(Photo by Dave Hopkins, courtesy of Dana Hopkins)*

Division of the U.S. Army. With the Cold War on, the Army was interested in locating sites for strategic airstrips in western Alaska. Army engineers thought the lava flows might provide a solid and permafrost-free substrate, but Hopkins saw the futility of the proposal with his first glance. Frost action during the cold stages of the Pleistocene epoch had fractured the gray-black basalt to form a rubble of angular blocks from a few feet in size to as much as twenty feet across. It didn't seem possible even to run a bulldozer over it, let alone an airplane. Nevertheless, it was still a good chance to study the history of the landscape on the Army's nickel. And Hopkins was eager to take an interdisciplinary approach in collaboration with Sigafoos.

Bob Sigafoos idolized Eric Hultén, the Swedish botanist who was then working on a compilation of the flora of Alaska, Yukon Territory, Kamchatka Peninsula, and northeastern Siberia. It was being published in twelve long installments by the Lund University in Sweden, each volume straightening out the taxonomy of a whole family. That kind of writing was almost impossible for Hopkins to read, but Sigafoos lived from issue to issue, devouring the pioneering work of the great scientist. He immediately put Hultén's articles to use as authoritative guides to identifying and classifying the tundra plants of northern Seward Peninsula. But Hopkins saw a bigger picture.

Hultén was a legend among Northern scientists, and Hopkins learned a bit about his life's story from a long letter Hultén sent him years later. In 1920, at the age of twenty-five, Hultén had gone to unexplored southern Kamchatka in the Russian Far East as botanist to a small expedition. Though the trip doubled as a honeymoon for Hultén and his bride, Elsie, it turned out to be something less than a pleasure cruise. It took nearly three months' travel—through Egypt, India, Singapore, Hong Kong, Shanghai, Yokohama—for the group to reach Hakodate, a port city on Japan's northernmost island. They decided not to pay the steep fare asked by the first schooner heading to the Kamchatka Peninsula, and it was just as well. Within days, that ship, loaded with gunpowder and gasoline, exploded.

Hultén's party did take passage on the next boat, the *Kommandor Bering*, which turned out to be the yacht of the former governor of Kamchatka. The governor, along with all officers and officials, had been recently executed during the ongoing Russian civil war, and the liberated yacht now carried the first Soviet governor of Kamchatka and other high

The *Kommandor Bering*, carrying twenty-six-year-old Eric Hultén and his wife Elsie, wrecked off Cape Lopatka, at the southern tip of Kamchatka Peninsula, Russia, 1920 *(Photo courtesy of Maj Hultén)*

officials. Unaccustomed to yachting, the Bolsheviks promptly piled the boat onto the rocks off the southern tip of Kamchatka. With the vessel listing sharply and taking on water, the crew managed to launch lifeboats, loaded with some provisions, and row everyone to the snowy beach. The next day, a storm broke up the yacht, and miscellaneous cargo washed ashore. The castaways had a camera but no film, guns but only bird shot. The area was so remote that there was no hope of reaching inhabited regions by foot. So the newlyweds set up a hut made from salvaged packing crates and, as the sanguine Hultén wrote elsewhere, "life in camp soon became quite bearable. We shot ducks and roasted them on spits, there was fish in the sea, the vodka flowed like water and all the signal rockets were used up in the merrymaking."

After about ten days, the shipwrecked party of Russians and Swedes sighted a Japanese steamer, which launched a boat. The captain refused help to anyone sailing on a Bolshevik-owned vessel, but he did agree to radio the Japanese fleet. After a few more days, two Japanese destroyers hove to in the heavy surf in front of the camp. Hultén's Japanese letters of introduction earned the Swedes passage to Petropavlovsk, but again the Russian revolutionaries were denied help. Only after some parleying did Hultén secure permission for the Russian governor to come along so that he could arrange for the rescue of the remainder of his stranded comrades.

The intrepid Hulténs set up their base of operations in Petropavlovsk, ranging outward on botanical collecting trips into the rugged hinterlands, now more dangerous than usual because it was also a combat zone. Once, they climbed to the top of Avatcha Volcano while doing their best to dodge skirmishing factions in the civil war. Sometimes they left town with the Bolsheviks presiding over city hall, then returned to find the Czarists in control. On horseback, with two native guides, they took extended trips through virgin country of "radiantly beautiful . . . park-like birch woods." Sometimes, they did not see anyone for months. Away from dangerous humans, they had only to contend with Kamchatkan brown bears lumbering through the underbrush. "Every week a bear was shot," wrote Hultén, "and bear and salmon, salmon and bear was the food for the day." Over the course of three years, they collected about twelve thousand plants, which set the Hulténs up with years of ambitious work in taxonomy and phytogeography (the study of the distribution of plants).

Between 1920 and 1922, Hultén and his wife conducted botanical field research in the wilderness of Kamchatka. They used horses in summer and skied in winter, with Hultén pulling a small sledge *(Photo courtesy of Maj Hultén)*

Hultén in Kamchatka: "Every week a bear was shot, and bear and salmon, salmon and bear was the food of the day" *(Photo courtesy of Maj Hultén)*

Luckily for budding Alaskan scientists like Hopkins and Sigafoos, Hultén's interests led him to another wild land on the Bering Sea, Alaska's Aleutian Islands. In the spring of 1932, at Unalaska, eight hundred miles west of Anchorage, he boarded a small fishing boat bound for Attu, the Aleutian island farthest west, another thousand miles distant. The captain of the *Eunice* allowed Hultén ashore whenever time and weather permitted. He climbed the steep volcanic mountainsides and collected "with great intensity," he wrote, "while the boat was drifting off-shore, waiting." Strong tides surged through the passes and straits, and there were no reliable navigational charts: "The only rule for navigation was not to sail into the kelp, the long algae covering the reefs." The little *Eunice* returned from Attu safely, and Hultén went on to publish his *Flora of the Aleutian Islands*. But that the voyage was risky is attested to by the fate of the *Eunice*. On her very next trip to Attu, she wrecked. All hands made shore, where all died of exposure.

Hultén began to publish the results of these researches as part of his doctoral dissertation at the University of Lund in 1937. It described the distribution of vascular plants between Canada's Mackenzie River and Siberia's Lena. When he plotted the ranges of several plants on the same map, he saw they took the shape of ovals, elongated in an east-west direction. Interestingly, the ovals tended to be concentric. He noted, too, a peculiar symmetry in the plants' ranges. The axis of symmetry was a line drawn through Bering Strait. "If they spread a little bit to the east of this line, they also spread a short way to the west of it. Should they spread far east, they also spread far west." Hultén suggested they were grouped around "centra," from which the plants must have radiated. And the central areas of radiation for various plants seemed to be not only in eastern Siberia and western Alaska, but also in the sea between.

When Hultén put this observation alongside what he knew of Ice Age conditions, a picture began to resolve itself in his mind. He knew that, when the ice sheets locked up much of the earth's water, the sea level must have fallen enough to expose the shallow continental shelf under the Bering and Chukchi Seas. Hultén imagined a dry landmass stretching from mostly unglaciated Siberia into mostly unglaciated Alaska. Cut off from the rest of North America by ice sheets, such a region would have been a great biological refugium, a place where Northern plants and animals survived extinction, and whence they evidently spread when the glaciers receded.

Picturing the Bering Strait region during the Ice Age, Hultén imagined his plant communities extending in unified ranges from west to east across an intercontinental landmass. It would have been a broad highway of biological exchange, with floral and faunal traffic moving in both directions. Though hypothetical and drowned for ten thousand years, the land bridge should have a name, Hultén thought. He christened it Beringia, after Vitus Bering, a fellow Scandinavian and the first recorded explorer to sail through the strait separating Asia and America. Today, scholars consider Beringia to be not just the presently submerged land bridge, but the unglaciated adjacent lands extending westward to at least the Kolyma River in Siberia and eastward to the Mackenzie River in Canada.

Aware of Hultén's Beringian hypothesis, Hopkins and his superiors at the U. S. Geological Survey thought a botanist might be a useful addition to his field party. Permafrost (permanently frozen ground) had just begun to be a subject of study for American soils engineers and geomorphologists, though there was already a substantial Russian literature. The Russians were showing relationships between vegetation types

After nearly three years of fieldwork in Kamchatka, Hultén, then twenty-eight, returned to Sweden for years of study of the collected plants. At thirty-six, he published *Flora of Kamchatka (Photo courtesy of Maj Hultén)*

and such soil characteristics as permafrost or the depth of seasonal thaw. Besides, Hopkins' superiors seemed to understand the value of simply dropping a good scientist into an area and giving him field support. He'll get interested in something, and the result will be useful. And that was how Bob Sigafoos, a botanist, came to be sitting in the lee of the wall tent at Hopkins' geological field camp at Lava Lake in the summer of 1948.

Sigafoos got interested in small-scale things, like studying the relation of vegetation to solifluction, how plants responded to frost-induced slope movement. This led to a paper, coauthored with Hopkins, that became a classic publication merging geology and botany: "Frost Action and Vegetation Patterns on Seward Peninsula." Sigafoos also got interested in big things, like the history of the position of the tree line. He extended Hultén's inquiries into the origin and history of the intricate mosaic of Arctic and subarctic plant cover. Like Hultén, Sigafoos was collecting plants, mapping their occurrence, and graphically overlaying the data to show the centers of Hultén's equiformal areas, points from which plants had dispersed, hence the locations of refugia during the glaciations. Advancing the work of his hero, Sigafoos was using the living plants to reconstruct the vanished landscape of Beringia. And Hopkins was there, absorbing it all, reveling in the cross-pollination that profited both parties, just as he knew it would.

On July 15, 1948, Hopkins' field crew moved enough of their gear from Lava Lake to establish a small satellite camp on another lake about twenty miles to the northeast, where the crew planned to map the geology. It was high up in the headwaters of Cottonwood Creek, which drained to the Goodhope River, which in turn flowed into the south shore of Kotzebue

Kuzutrin Lake camp, 1948, showing Bob Sigafoos, eight-by-ten wall tents, and smaller sleeping tents
*(Photo by Dave Hopkins, courtesy of Dana Hopkins)*

Sound. Hopkins named it Cloud Lake because, often as not, the lake was inside a cloud. "Every cloud within 50 miles passed over us," he wrote home, "and every one of them dragged its bottom over the lake." On days that were merely cloudy everywhere else, he said, Cloud Lake was lashed with wind and fog and drizzle. The wind never blew less than twenty miles per hour, and seldom less than thirty. The men wore wool underwear, wool shirts, wool sweaters, and rubberized rain parkas. Because the camp was on a sandy beach, when the wind wasn't blowing rain, it was blowing sand. "I had sand in my sleeping bag," he wrote, "sand in my shoes, sand in my hair, sand in all of the guns, sand in my coffee, sand in my hot-cakes, and sand in my soup."

In the evening, all five men crowded into the eight-by-eight tent for dinner. For a bridge table, they spread a newspaper over a packboard. Seitz sat on a box of C-rations, Fernald on a gas can, and Hopkins and Sigafoos shared an air mattress. Sigafoos had an old reindeer skull for a backrest. Leaning back into it and fanning his cards, the curving antlers serving for his armrests, he must have looked like a Pleistocene chieftain consulting his magic. "It was a picture," Hopkins wrote, "the five of us dirty and bearded—Bill sitting and cursing the stove or walking over the card table to go outdoors for food or water from the lake; Inmachuk poking his nose in the tent, trying to come in and add to the congestion."

Hopkins went on to catalogue the artifacts of the crew's material culture. On the floor were the stove, food, Quay's sleeping bag and clothes, dead birds and lemming skins piled in with the food, pickled lemmings, owl pellets, and a can of dead snails. Against the amber canvas of the tent walls were a box of specimens, an ancient Eskimo wood implement, a rifle, two shotguns, and two fishing rods. In every other spot, wet clothes hung like bats, respiring steamy vapors, releasing an occasional dropping and imparting a dank redolence to the close space.

Camping at remote lakes on Seward Peninsula in the 1940s wasn't always comfortable, but it was almost always interesting. For instance, there was the occasional visit from John Cross, the bush pilot who had been ferrying the crew and their gear from lake to lake with his odd looking, four-seat amphibious Seabee, powered by a single, rear-mounted pusher engine. Cross liked to drop from the sky and splash the bulbous fuselage down onto the lake in front of the camp and invite himself up to the cook tent for coffee and a chat. Hopkins was as

Eskimo children at Deering, 1948 *(Photo by Dave Hopkins, courtesy of Dana Hopkins)*

enthralled with the bush pilot as he had been with Frank Gage of the Boston & Maine Railroad.

Cross was an independent operator based at Deering, where he lived with his wife, an Eskimo woman named Bessie Barr, and their three children. He had such a soft-spoken, serious, and understated manner that he seemed incapable of exaggeration. Hopkins thought of him as a sort of scholar without books. He paid attention to nature, then put things together for himself. And this knowledge—his interpretation of the natural world—he organized into stories. Still, his stories were so amazing that Hopkins could never be completely sure about them. One day when the party was camped at Imuruk Lake, Cross mentioned that if the scientists were studying Seward Peninsula's prehistory, they might be interested to know that there were arrowheads in some caves over on Trail Creek, up near the lake the men were calling Cloud Lake. Hopkins definitely was interested.

It's bear country, though, said Cross offhandedly. A fellow would want to bring along a rifle if he was going to go poking up those brushy ravines. A couple of miners from Candle were over there a few years ago. It turned stormy on them, so they figured they'd duck into one of those caves on Trail Creek. But they started thinking there might be bears in there. Well, these men were prospectors, said Cross, so they had dynamite with them. They threw a stick in there to scare the bear out. Sure enough, a grizzly came charging out, not one bit happy. Well, OK. They were ready for that. But as they were dealing with him, another bear charged out of the cave. They pretty much had their hands full with two grizzly bears, when they look up

Bush pilot John Cross and his Seabee on Kuzitrin Lake, 1948
*(Photo by Dave Hopkins, courtesy of Dana Hopkins)*

to see a third bear roaring down on them. But there *were* arrowheads in there all right. Bones, too. Sipping his coffee, the bush pilot gave his listeners to understand that, if they planned to go hiking up Trail Creek, they'd want to bring their rifles.

Hopkins could not be certain whether Cross's story—three bears in one cave, and the dynamite-tossing miners—was completely believable, but he got a glimpse of the caves once when Cross was able to fly him over Trail Creek. He was determined to explore the caves, and on the twenty-second of July, everyone but Sigafoos took off on a forty-mile spike trip that would take them down Cottonwood Creek to Trail Creek, up Trail Creek to the caves, then downstream to the mouth of Cottonwood Creek, and back by way of the Right Fork of the Goodhope River. It didn't exactly rain the first day, though the willows conspired to collect the heavy mist, merging the atomized water and funneling it down to the point of each creased leaf. There it hung in fat droplets until it could be conveniently transferred to the clothing of the men pushing through.

Still, it was beautiful country. Cottonwood Creek flowed through a canyon with six-hundred-foot lava-topped cliffs on the south bank and rugged limestone ridges on the north side. As the men descended along game trails through steep-walled cut banks at the bottom of the canyon, each bend opened up new views. Here and there, the creek widened into a small flood plain where pleasant groves of fifteen-foot willows grew. The mists that hung on the cliffs above finally lifted, and the sun lit up a sparkling green valley. On the north wall, a family of eagles circled the eroded core of an ancient cinder cone as if tethered to it. That night, camping by the creek, Hopkins slid into his sleeping bag with wet long johns, hoping they would dry by morning. But he stayed awake until twelve-thirty, noting all these details in a letter addressed as usual to his parents, but with the knowledge that it would be shared with Mrs. Gage (the station agent's wife), Lucy Brooks (the librarian), Nellie Mason (the post mistress), and paraphrased to the members of the Rotary Club who asked after him.

The men reached the mouth of Trail Creek the next day, just as a rain shower caught up with them. Through the boiling fog, they could just see the limestone cliffs. With great caution, Hopkins led the way. He circled high on the valley walls to avoid the thick brush, shotgun at the ready, a slug in the chamber. At the first cave, they sent the dog, Chuk, up to investigate. When nothing happened, they pulled the fireworks from their packs—not dynamite, but Fourth of July skyrockets and Roman candles purchased in Nome. With a burst of fire and smoke, the rocket roared into the cave, careening off the rocks inside and filling the interior with sparks, flashes, and a loud, echoing racket. Smoke poured out, but no bears. Finally, they lit their carbide lamps and crawled in. For the first thirty feet or so, the cave was between two and three feet high and six feet wide. Then it opened to a room about nine feet wide, twelve feet long, and high enough for them to sit upright. Beyond the room, the tunnel narrowed in both dimensions for another thirty feet before terminating at a solid wall of ice. They saw that wolves had used the room, as dung and chewed reindeer bones attested. They found the leg bone of a bear, a bone implement, and a sardine can.

At the second of the four large caves, the men were bolder. After having Chuk sniff the entrance, they lit their lamps and crawled in. They were more than a little optimistic about the cave's archeological potential, half expecting to find early man artifacts sitting in plain view on the floor of the caves. Not only were these not evident, but the dirt was frozen immediately below the surface, eliminating the possibility of a test excavation.

Hopkins left Quay to dig a small pit outside the entrance of the most interesting cave while he and the others climbed the rocks to check out some of the smaller holes. In their separate pursuits, each party verified aspects of John Cross's stories. Hopkins' gaze fell on a hump of overturned sod across the valley when suddenly it moved. He judged the grizzly to be a little smaller than a house.

Meanwhile, Quay unearthed a beautiful red-brown, jasper lance point. This artifact looked like what was at that time called a Yuma point, Hopkins thought, hence an example of one of the earliest cultures then known to exist in the New World. Back at the Cloud Lake camp, Hopkins laid the point out on a piece of cloth and photographed it. Then he packed it for shipment home. He decided that he would write up a short paper on the Trail Creek find. He'd send it to Louis Giddings, the Alaskan archeologist whom he had been dying to meet.

A week later, the crew packed up their Cloud Lake camp and flew back to the bosom of their nicely outfitted base camp at Lava Lake. Hopkins thought back on Cloud Lake as the prettiest place they had yet camped—and the most miserable. "I wasn't warm once in the last two weeks," he wrote home. But now they all took baths, trimmed their beards, and washed their dirty clothes. They had a table on which to eat and play bridge. When the sun broke through the clouds, they hung their damp clothes and sleeping bags out to dry, cleaned the guns, sharpened knives, and "rubbed the soot off the dirtier of the dishes." Then the young scientists sat in the sun and caught up on their notes.

It was freezing at night, now, as August advanced. Instead of rain, wet snow pellets blew in on the wind. Restless birds began to aggregate. The sandpipers flocked up and left. High overhead, easier to hear than to see, a long, fluttering V of

Sigafoos, Quay, and Hopkins dry gear and wait for an airplane at Lava Lake, 1948 *(Courtesy of Dana Hopkins)*

geese moved purposefully south. It was as if an invisible airplane had snagged the great strand in the middle and was towing it across the sky, advertising winter to the world below. The terns, the snipes, and the ducks disappeared. And now the cranes were flocking up at Lava Lake. In groups of a dozen or more they glided in, landing on the tundra on the north side. They stalked around, studies in rectitude, welcoming incoming brethren with deafening, unearthly, and earsplitting croaks, like the sound of a thousand pterodactyls strangling. As the flock grew larger, a handful of cranes began to jump and hop, inciting other birds until waves rippled through the crowd. When a hundred or more birds had gathered, the energy could not be contained. The center could not hold. The entire agglomeration rose, boiling and churning, like the early stages of a nuclear explosion. Scattered and inchoate at first, the cranes began to coalesce into small whirlwinds, which in turn merged and condensed as the birds wound themselves into a proper cyclone of biomass and commotion, rounding and wheeling and rising, auguring themselves into the sky until they were nearly invisible—like flecks of nutmeg swirled into a fluffy batter. When they seemed ready to disappear altogether into the white cumulus, the specks arranged themselves into perfect formation and, like a defiant compass arrow, shot away to the south.

# 6
# Something Going On

Joan (pronounced Jo-Ann) Prewitt was a pretty, dark-haired twenty-year-old at Radcliffe College when she told Dave Hopkins, whom she'd been dating for some time, "There's something going on between us." Hopkins had sense enough to realize that the something was love and that he had been tendered "a sort of put up or shut up proposition," as he says. They were married in New Mexico, where Joan had grown up on a ranch not only larger than Gypson's Woods, but, Hopkins was amazed to learn, probably larger than all of Greenfield Township.

Joan had both a love of outdoor work and training in geology (she would earn a master's degree from Radcliffe-Harvard). In the summer of 1950, she accompanied Dave on his field research trip to Alaska. They had the use of a surplus Army weasel, a light amphibious track vehicle powered by a six-cylinder Studebaker engine. On Joan's twenty-first birthday they ran the weasel out to Cape Douglas, crossing the coastal plain and the old beach ridges. Hopkins shot a picture of Joan sitting on a giant boulder in front of the wave-cut limestone cliffs of an ancient beach, now high and dry. Once, when the tide was out, they took the weasel along the beach around the coast to the Eskimo village of Teller. For miles, there were only cliffs on one side and the sea on the other. They suddenly

Raised on a ranch in New Mexico, Joan Prewitt Hopkins earned a master's degree in geology from Radcliffe-Harvard and assisted her husband for two summers in Alaska *(Courtesy of Dana Hopkins)*

realized that if the weasel were to break down, they would die with the rising tide. The Studebaker engine chugged faithfully onward, however, and they made Teller, reminded of the Arctic's capacity to claim the ultimate price for carelessness, and resolved never again to be so foolish.

Joan worked with her husband for two summers in Alaska, returning with him to Washington, D.C., each fall, where Hopkins worked in the USGS's Terrain and Permafrost Section. He felt two ways about living in Washington. He enjoyed the bookstores, especially the Washington Book Shop on Connecticut Avenue, where he attended parties and leftist lectures and heard Pete Seeger perform. He joined the United Federal Workers, which, he says, "was rather a left CIO union—and not just 'rather.'" He was troubled by the racial discrimination he'd seen in the workplace and worked on grievances filed with the union. "In those days, black people only worked as elevator operators and messengers. Jews couldn't be put in positions where they'd be working over non-Jews. So, promotions for almost anybody other than WASPS were very difficult." Though these activities invigorated him, Hopkins found the D.C. winters dreary. Both he and Joan wanted to move west.

After the 1951–52 field season, Hopkins contrived to work for a month on an Alaska geologic mapping project at USGS's Alaska Branch, then located in the old U.S. Mint building in downtown San Francisco. He and Joan, who now had a baby daughter, stayed with Clyde Wharhaftig in his apartment on Telegraph Hill overlooking the bay. Clyde had been Hopkins' grad school roommate, a frequent guest in the family home in Greenfield, and best man at his wedding. Now the two best friends worked together. Every day they'd walk down Grant Avenue, through the Italian neighborhood of North Beach with its spaghetti factories and beatnik coffee houses and on through Chinatown, where the shopkeepers would be setting out vegetables on sidewalk stands. They turned up Market Street, crossing at the foot of Powell, where the clanging cable cars turned around on a big wooden turntable; and strode down Fifth to Mission Street, entering the USGS offices in the stately old U.S. Mint building. Colleagues in the Alaska Branch called Hopkins and Wharhaftig "The Gold Dust Twins," because they had "gold-plated" diplomas (doctorates from Harvard), they had been to the gold fields of Alaska, and they were inseparable. When the temporary assignment ended, however, Hopkins returned to Washington and the Terrain and Permafrost Section.

The San Francisco–based Alaska Branch operated with considerable autonomy, almost like a miniature USGS, and that appealed to Hopkins. He applied for permanent assignment there, and, when the chance came in December 1954, he packed up his family and drove cross-country. It poured rain through central California, but as they reached the Dumbarton Bridge and crossed San Francisco Bay into Menlo Park, where the USGS had new offices, it poured sunshine. It was January 1, 1955, and everything was wet and sparkling. The air was fresh, the acacias were blooming, the birds singing—even the year was new. "It looked," said Hopkins, "as though I had arrived in Paradise."

The couple bought an old farmhouse in the Los Altos hills on five acres with apricot and plum trees, a walnut and a lemon tree. Joan reclaimed the gardens and trees and worked through a list of remodeling chores. She also did volunteer work for progressive political causes and candidates. Early in their marriage, she had gravitated toward her husband's social and political philosophy, and, as Hopkins became more absorbed in his profession, "Joan became more and more my social conscience," as he wrote a friend. It was more than that, he said, "she was my spark plug and steering wheel." When she gave birth to a second daughter, Joan's mother came to stay while Hopkins went off to the Seward Peninsula for another field season. It was during that time, while he was visiting various placer deposits around Nome, that a message from Joan's mother finally caught up with him. It said simply: "Come home."

When he reached a phone and called his mother-in-law, she would not, or perhaps could not, tell him what was the matter, but gave him the phone number of a doctor. Hopkins still remembers the first words he heard when the doctor got on the line: "Mr. Hopkins I'm awfully sorry we didn't catch this in time."

Cancer.

A grieving Hopkins at Manley Hot Springs in Interior Alaska in 1956 *(Courtesy of Dave Hopkins)*

More than forty years later, at the age of seventy-seven, Hopkins sat one day sifting through a box of photographs, happily annotating them with his memories. Opening one folder, he quickly closed it up and replaced it in the box. The pictures were of a young family in a sunny yard beside a farmhouse. His old eyes filled with tears, and he waited a few moments until he could get control of his voice. "That was when Joan was sick," he whispered. "I can't look at them now."

Joan Prewitt Hopkins was twenty-seven.

While recovering from a disastrously incompatible second marriage, Hopkins attended the sort of encounter group common in the San Francisco area in the 1960s. There he met and eventually married Rachel Chouinard, a pretty, French Canadian woman with an easygoing nature and a lively sense of humor. Though Hopkins was in the field for months at a time each year, Rachel maintained not just a home for their combined family of six, but a group foster home that sometimes brought the total to eleven.

# GIDDINGS

When the tide is out, there is just enough beach on the outer face of Cape Denbigh for a pilot who knows what he's doing to land a light airplane. Moreover, when he sheds the weight of his passenger and cargo, he has a reasonable chance of taking off again. Art Johnson, a bush pilot operating out of the Eskimo village of Shaktoolik, knew what he was doing. As he dropped in from the north, his passenger, Hopkins, saw nothing but four-hundred-foot cliffs out the left window and nothing but breaking waves out the right. But Johnson had circled first. He had estimated the length of the beach at about a thousand feet and noted that it terminated abruptly in a steep cliff. He had gauged the size of the cobbles he would be landing on—about the size of softballs. And he'd checked the waves to figure that the wind was out of the south. Johnson dropped the plane in from the north, set it down safely, then turned and jounced back to the north end of the beach.

After Hopkins piled out with his gear, Johnson asked him to grab the plane's tail and dig in his heels. When the engine whined and the prop wash blew hard in his face and the tail began to rise and tug, Hopkins let go. The little plane seemed to burst out of his hand like a released bird. He watched it run up the beach in a great roar and panic, the way a red-throated loon takes off, with its windmilling legs pattering wildly across the surface of the water until its flapping wings get a bite on the air. Once sufficiently aloft to clear a wing, the plane banked sharply across the face of the cliff, rose, banked again around the headland and was gone. Johnson had offered to pick him up at the same beach, but "after watching him take off," Hopkins wrote in a letter, "I made darn sure that I got back to Shaktoolik by boat."

From the air, Hopkins had gotten a good look at the Reindeer Hills. It was a fist of high ground at the end of an arm of swampy lowland separating Norton Bay from its namesake sound. Cape Denbigh protruded southward from the fist like the thumb of a merciless emperor. On the seaward side of the fist, in what would be the indentation between the middle knuckles, is the place the local people call Iyatayet. Art Johnson had buzzed Louis Giddings' camp at Iyatayet before setting Hopkins down on the beach a mile away. In bush Alaska, the low pass is equivalent to ringing the doorbell. Giddings dispatched his Eskimo helpers to pick up the visitor, and pretty soon Hopkins was skimming across the water in a boat sheathed with the skins of ooguruk (bearded seal). Rounding a cliff, he saw the little inlet where Iyatayet Creek tumbled out of the hills and slid across the beach into the sea. Beside the stream were four white canvas wall tents, and, on a grassy terrace forty feet above the left bank, he saw the fresh dirt that marked Giddings' latest excavation.

Though his greatest discoveries were ahead of him, by 1950 Louis Giddings had already made a mark in Alaska. Hopkins, at least, had been hearing stories about the half-legendary Giddings for years. In Palmer in the early forties when Hopkins was mapping coal deposits in the Matanuska Valley, he used to run into a fellow named Jack Newcomb at The

Hopkins at Louis Giddings' excavation at Iyatayet Creek, Cape Denbigh *(Courtesy of Haffenreffer Museum, Brown University)*

Lodge. Newcomb was in the Alaska Scouts, a military unit famous for its outdoor skills. He had worked occasionally as an archeological assistant, and would mesmerize listeners—especially Hopkins—with stories of the intrepid Louie Giddings.

Giddings was a tall, soft-spoken Texan who took epic trips across rugged country, sometimes prospecting for gold and sometimes for archeological remains. As one of Giddings' professors wrote years later, "I remember him each spring going off into the wilderness alone, equipped with a bed roll, some small bags of rice and raisins and a .22 rifle to shoot the ground squirrels upon which he would live for months." After graduating from the University of Alaska in 1931, Giddings spent five summers working for a mining outfit that washed away the overburden of silt with hydraulic "giants." But another kind of buried treasure intrigued Giddings: ancient spruce wood that the hoses uncovered at various levels in the muck. Attempting to date the samples, Giddings worked out his own (ultimately impractical) method of tree ring analysis. Eventually, he wrote the inventor of dendrochronology, the astronomer Andrew Douglass, at the University of Arizona. Shortly, Douglass was sponsoring the promising student's graduate study in Tucson.

While his master's degree progressed, Giddings did fieldwork in Alaska and worked for the University of Alaska's anthropology department. In 1939, he assisted Froelich Rainey and Helge Larsen in excavating the Ipiutak house pits at Point Hope, a find that had pushed Eskimo history back a thousand years. It was one of the great discoveries of the Arctic world, an unexpected prehistoric Eskimo culture notable for fantastic and intricate ivory carving and engraving. Hopkins remembers being just out of high school when *National Geographic* magazine ran a big spread on the spectacular find. "I was thrilled by it and began to think about meeting these mighty explorers some day."

When Giddings thought about how the ancient people made a living at the end of a spit that jutted fifteen miles into the sea, he suspected they might have lived in the settlement only during the summer, where they hunted seals and walrus, then moved inland after freeze-up to hunt caribou. To test his theory and to work on a tree ring chronology, he wanted to look for sites along the Kobuk River that stretched inland from Kotzebue.

Giddings' idea was to fly into the Athabascan Indian village of Allakaket on the Koyukuk River, a tributary of the Yukon, then hike west over a low pass to the Kobuk. On reaching the river, he planned to build a raft and float down toward the Chukchi Sea. He mentioned the plan to the University of Alaska's longtime president, Charles Bunnell, who told him it was definitely unwise to attempt a trip of that length alone in totally uninhabited country. Giddings let the matter drop for a time, but he found he couldn't shake the idea. He figured he could do it and thought a field party "needlessly costly," even "encumbering." He preferred to travel light, as he wrote in his classic memoir *Ancient Men of the Arctic*, "resting when I pleased, day or night, and accountable to no one."

In July 1940, Giddings flew to Allakaket, which sits astride the Arctic Circle. From there, it is about ninety miles to the Kobuk River, with no trail markings and no settlements along the way. Fifty of those miles between the two rivers were simply uncharted, a blank space on Giddings' USGS map. He took a light pack: a tent, a down sleeping bag, rain gear, and a change of heavy long johns (mainly for protection against mosquitoes). With respect to edible provisions, he was likewise unencumbered, depending on a .22 rifle, some fishing line, and flies.

At Allakaket, the horrified missionaries made it clear they opposed Giddings' foolhardy plan. The last person to attempt the trip, they said, had never been heard from again. When Giddings waved good-by and headed up the Alatna River, the missionaries sent off an urgent letter to President Bunnell saying that, if Giddings didn't return to Allakaket fairly soon, Bunnell should organize an air search.

The Alatna teemed with ducks, and along its shores Giddings ate well and enjoyed himself. When he judged he had gone far enough north, he adjusted his compass to follow a straight line west. From here to the Kobuk, he would have to rely on shooting squirrels and birds, and catching fish in the one sizable stream he would cross. Leaving the river, Giddings headed west into the soggy muskeg, stirring up swarms of mosquitoes.

> The ordeal of the following three days made me keenly aware of the difficulties Indians had long faced in hot interior summers. For hours at a time no breath of air disturbed the cloud of mosquitoes that surrounded me. Although I wore my head net continuously, I nevertheless had to plug the air holes in my hat and anchor the net securely to the front of my shirt to prevent the buzzing, probing insects from finding every weak spot in my armor. If I sat to rest, so that the insulation of clothing tightened over shoulder or knee, some few of these small swordsmen unfailingly managed to thrust their weapons deep enough to draw blood. Walking hour after hour with or without the hot July sun, I perspired until my entire soggy costume grew saturated. ... Small gnats, "no see-ums," and larger ones, "bulldogs," found a way into, under, or through my head net, biting at leisure or flying blindly into my eyes.

Giddings hit the Kobuk exactly where he expected. Without ax or hatchet, he set about building a raft. He had intended to lash driftwood logs together with willow stems but found he could pin them together by using his tree borer as a drill, whittling pegs, and, like a Stone Age man, pounding them home with a rock. For three days, he floated down the Kobuk, periodically disturbing ducks and black bears from their fishing. He himself fished at the mouths of creeks and gorged on berries where he found them. Sixty miles downriver, he approached the fish camp of a Native family. When the people spotted him, they ran terrified into their tents and tied up the flaps behind them. The little raft had become so waterlogged that it was almost completely submerged. The white man seemed to come around the bend standing up in the middle of the river, no boat under him at all.

For the next three weeks, Giddings located and excavated archeological sites on the upper Kobuk, then bought a canvas-covered kayak from a Native man and worked his way another one hundred sixty miles downriver to the Eskimo village of Kiana, where he caught a boat to Kotzebue and a plane to Fairbanks. As word spread, professional archeologists marveled at Giddings' accomplishment. Alone, and without institutional support, he had just completed a pioneering archeological survey of one of the most remote regions of Alaska.

After wartime service in the Navy, Giddings returned to study the Arctic woodland cultures. Over several years, he excavated seventy-three houses at twelve sites. In 1948, he was preparing to survey the shores of Norton Sound for sites that he might relate to Kobuk River cultures when a letter arrived from his former assistant, Jack Newcomb, the fellow Hopkins had met in The Lodge in Palmer. Newcomb now taught school in Shaktoolik on Norton Sound and was writing to tell Giddings of two nearby archeological sites he'd discovered. Giddings flew directly to Shaktoolik.

Looking over both sites, Giddings considered that surface leavings at each place indicated fairly recent occupation. His hunch was that the site the Eskimos called Nukleet, near the tip of Cape Denbigh, might be more promising than the place they called Iyatayet, ten miles away. He settled down and dug a test trench at Nukleet. But he was puzzled by the fact that at Nukleet nearly all the tools were of polished slate, while at Iyatayet flinty flakes were common on the surface of the ground. "Could there be," Giddings wrote later, "at [Iyatayet], beneath a veneer of late occupation, the leavings of some people who, like those of Ipiutak, had preferred flints to slate?" As soon as the test trench at Nukleet was finished, Giddings moved camp to Iyatayet.

Working alone one day at Iyatayet, Giddings lifted the wooden floor of a sod house ruin probably occupied in the 1600s. Beneath it he found pottery shards, stone lamps, and chipped stone implements, some of which reminded him of Ipiutak artifacts considered to be two thousand or more years old. Below that level he found nothing but sandy silt. To be sure there were no more cultural layers, he continued painstakingly to trowel into the sterile, undisturbed soil. When it had become obvious that the excavation had reached its conclusion, Giddings, for some reason, poked the tip of his trowel into the soil to test the depth of thaw. Immediately, he felt the gritty resistance of flinty material. Using the trowel like a cake knife, he tipped out an intact slice of the compacted silt. Glittering underneath were countless tiny flakes of obsidian and chert and the glistening prismatic facets of microblades and projectile points. Giddings saw at once that they resembled the Middle Stone Age artifacts found in Europe. He was the first person to see anything like it in America.

There were large Yuma points similar to those found at Paleo-Indian sites in the American west. And there were hundreds of slivers of chalcedony, chert, and obsidian. These flakes had been chipped away to sharpen tools called burins, used for cutting or grooving antler and ivory. The delicate craftsmanship of the Denbigh people was especially evident in microblades. Barely more than an inch long but carefully flaked in parallel diagonal rows, they could be fit into slots grooved along the sides of weapon shafts. Giddings' find at Iyatayet rewrote Eskimo archeology. Burins, for example, had not previously been found in America, and microblades were very rare. They were the most singular feature both of the Denbigh people's tool kit and of ten-thousand-year-old cultures found in the Gobi Desert of Asia. Giddings believed that the Denbigh Flint complex, as he named the oldest layer of artifacts, was similarly ancient, though later work proved otherwise. Still, he had pushed back the antiquity of Eskimo culture to about five thousand years and established a connection between Old and New World cultures.

It was the jasper lance point that Hopkins had found at Trail Creek Caves that led to his first meeting with Louie Giddings and the invitation to visit Iyatayet. Hopkins had wrapped the point carefully for shipping to his office in the States. But in those days a package sent by air from Nome to a destination in the Lower Forty-eight might sit in Wien Airlines' hangar in Fairbanks for weeks awaiting space on a southbound plane. Hopkins' package was gathering dust when the building burned down. The jasper point was lost. Fortunately, he had sketched and photographed the artifact. On a trip through Fairbanks, with sketch and photo, maps and notes, Hopkins hiked one evening up to the log cabin on the University of Alaska campus where Louis Giddings and his wife, Bets, lived. The cabin, which still stands today, was built in the late 1930s by Giddings' professor at the University of Alaska, Froelich Rainey. At that time, it was set well away from the other buildings, on a south-facing ridge with a view of the Tanana Flats all the way to the Alaska Range. Today it is flanked by dormitories, and the view is obscured by a stand of tall aspen trees that cover the slope.

Hopkins says he had been "just waiting for an adequate opportunity—an excuse, actually," to meet Giddings. Decades later, he sat for an interview in the same log cabin on the University of Alaska campus, recalling the welcome he received there from Giddings and his wife: "What I remember was a very warm experience. The warm color of the logs which we can still see, the blazing fire in the fireplace, and also the warmth of Louis and Bets Giddings themselves."

Giddings was a dozen years older than Hopkins. But, unlike Hopkins, who seemed always to be on the accelerated plan, always a couple years younger than his classmates, Giddings' ascendancy was gradual. Like many University of Alaska students (then and now), he was older than the standard cohort and in possession of life experiences beyond schools. He was taking his time with his education, and never seemed completely sure if his preference was to pursue graduate studies or just to take off and go prospecting. He didn't earn his master's degree until nine years after graduating from college, and would not earn his doctorate for ten more years. But even if Hopkins at twenty-seven and Giddings at thirty-nine were at approximately the same stage of formal education, Giddings was already a notable figure in Arctic science. He had been visiting the Bering Strait region since 1934 and was the first person to apply dendrochronology to the Arctic. Finding that rings in Arctic trees were more sensitive to temperature than to precipitation, he worked out the first long-term record of ancient climate in the American Arctic. Applying this timeline to the wood found in ancient dwellings, he became the first person to precisely date prehistoric archeological sites in Alaska. Now he had just discovered the oldest known traces of Eskimo culture at Iyatayet.

Giddings was excited about Hopkins' Trail Creek Caves discoveries. But he was also eager to get back to his own work at Iyatayet and couldn't take on another project. He suggested that Hopkins send him a report of his test excavations at Trail Creek. Hopkins did so, and Giddings sent it on to his friend Helge Larsen in Denmark, offering him the chance to excavate what he recognized as the only known cave site in Alaska. Larsen was happy to do so.

As the field season of 1949 approached, Hopkins wrote Giddings that he "would like very much to visit you, if it can be done without inconveniencing you too much." Giddings replied, "It would mean a lot to me to have you look over the site." He hoped that a geologist could puzzle out the origin and age of the flint-bearing soils. But as things worked out, Hopkins' own fieldwork prevented a visit to Iyatayet during the summer of 1949, though he did manage to visit Larsen at Trail Creek for a day in August. Larsen and his crew excavated the caves that summer and the next, collecting a wide variety of artifacts and bones. Near the surface were arrowheads of fairly recent cultures, extending back perhaps a thousand years. Beneath that were arrowheads and side blades similar to those found at Ipiutak. Lower still, they came upon obliquely flaked spear points like the one Hopkins' party had excavated, apparently related to similar points from the American Southwest. At the deepest layer, Larsen found arrowheads and flints similar to the oldest artifacts Giddings was turning up at Iyatayet. He also unearthed antler projectile points cut with grooves on opposite sides, apparently to accept razor-sharp microblade insets, the only such find in Eastern Beringia. Larsen thought the artifacts might be eight thousand to ten thousand years old.

Now, a year later, as Hopkins jumped out of the skin boat at Iyatayet beach, Giddings was especially glad he'd come. He took Hopkins up to the excavation and explained the trouble he was having understanding the stratigraphy of the site, which should have been the key to dating it. As Giddings spoke in his Texas drawl, using his shovel as a pointer, Hopkins thought he was a wonder. He looked like a cowboy in archeologists' clothes, speaking the archeologists' language, the very embodiment of the outdoorsman/scholar he'd imagined since boyhood. The layer of Denbigh Flint culture artifacts, Giddings said, did not always lie parallel to the surface. Sometimes the flint layer bulged and curved like a wave. It showed up clearly in cross section, traced on the pit walls that were parallel to the slope of the hill. Here, the ancient layer of flints sometimes folded over itself, like an S, even though the soil layers above it might lie more or less parallel to the surface. What was going on?

Hopkins jumped down in the trench and probed in the dirt. It didn't take long for him to recognize the geologic processes involved and explain it to Giddings. He and Bob Sigafoos had been studying the phenomenon on Seward Peninsula. Nevertheless, he was amazed to find that Giddings, used to working on a much finer scale, had prepared terrifically detailed drawings of the folds. Hopkins explained the process called solifluction. In the spring, on a slope underlain with permafrost, the upper layers of soil can thaw and become saturated with surface melt. Where saturation, steepness, and soil conditions favor it, this material can creep downslope as a lobe. The layer bearing the cultural material may be thawed in some upslope places, but frozen downslope. Thawed sections can slide downhill and override still frozen and immobile lower sections, producing the S-shaped strand. It is something like a miniature underground landslide, soil folding over itself underneath the surface, sometimes visible on the surface as an uphill slump and a downhill bulge. Surface deposits over time may add to the soil depth, burying the S-shaped layer deep underground. That was how Giddings found the Denbigh layer at Iyatayet.

As Hopkins and Giddings began to synthesize the archeological and geological evidence at the site, they found they could infer ancient fluctuations in climate and sea level, and speculate as to the age of the oldest artifacts. The paper they coauthored on the topic was one of the earliest attempts to relate archeological sequences to geologic and climactic chronologies. As it happened, their best guess was off by a few thousand years. But the advantages of interdisciplinary collaboration were not only reinforced in Hopkins' mind but also demonstrated to the scientific world. From then on the two great Arctic scientists became friends, correspondents, and consultants to each other.

Giddings, too, moved between disciplines. His first scientific specialization, dendrochronology, is a technique that begins where counting tree rings leaves off. Besides the *number* of

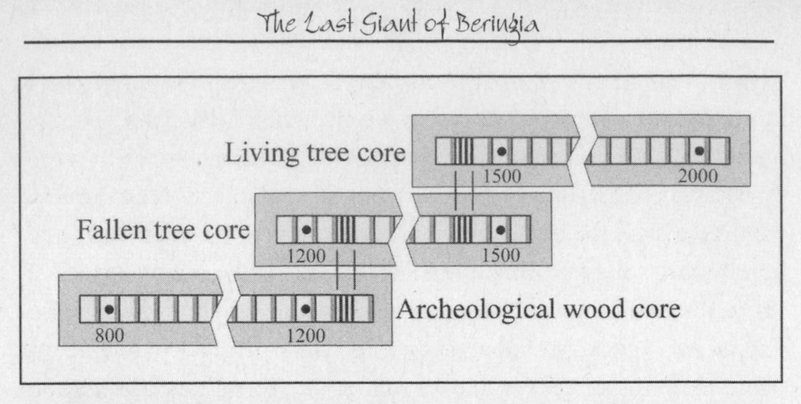


Stylized tree ring cores depicting cross-dating of living trees and wooden remains *(Courtesy of the Laboratory of Tree Ring Research, University of Arizona)*

annual growth rings, the *size* of the rings offers information. Favorable weather conditions produce more growth, hence wider rings. When conditions are less favorable, growth is retarded, and the rings are comparatively thinner. So, a given tree will have a sequence of rings of varying thicknesses. When a tree is cored, the ring pattern can be read—like a bar code—to identify the particular sequence of years during which the tree lived. Trees of the same age, from the same region, would have similar sequences of wide and narrow rings. But even trees of widely different ages can be aligned if their lifespans overlap. One simply matches up the portions of the cores where the sequence is the same. The first fifty years of a living three hundred-year-old tree, for example, may overlap with the last fifty years of a tree that lived for five hundred years, then was toppled and became a house post. By aligning the rings that match, a continuous sequence can be obtained for the last seven hundred fifty years (three hundred plus five hundred years, less fifty because of the overlap). When the rings of an even older piece of wood can be matched with those of the house post, the record is extended back farther.

Like pasting together a mosaic of overlapping photographs shot in a panoramic sequence, a tree ring pattern can be extended backward indefinitely. Ancient ridgepoles, rafters, tool handles, and charred bits of firewood can be cored and matched. Working from the living trees and wood from old Eskimo village sites on the Kobuk River, Giddings established a tree ring chronology for the last one thousand years.

Perhaps it was Giddings' habit of seeing in ripples the passage of time that worked on his mind as he looked down from small airplanes onto arrays of old beaches around Bering Strait during the 1950s. At Choris Peninsula on Kotzebue Sound, he saw old beach ridges parallel to the shore and extending inland in ranks. Between the ridges ran swales, sometimes collecting so much water that they looked like canals. Digging on one of these beach ridges, he discovered huge oval house pits—up to thirty-nine feet in length—that contained some of the earliest pottery found along that coast.

A prograding, or advancing, beach like the one at Choris grows as sand is washed from an eroding beach and transported along the shore by the currents. Eventually, a large storm or high spring tides with strong onshore winds will drive the surplus sand and gravel to shore and heap the material into a ridge just below the temporarily elevated sea level. When the sea falls again after the storm, a new ridge stands above the shoreline, like a new ring added to the outside of a tree. Giddings identified nine beach ridges at Choris Peninsula. Since the

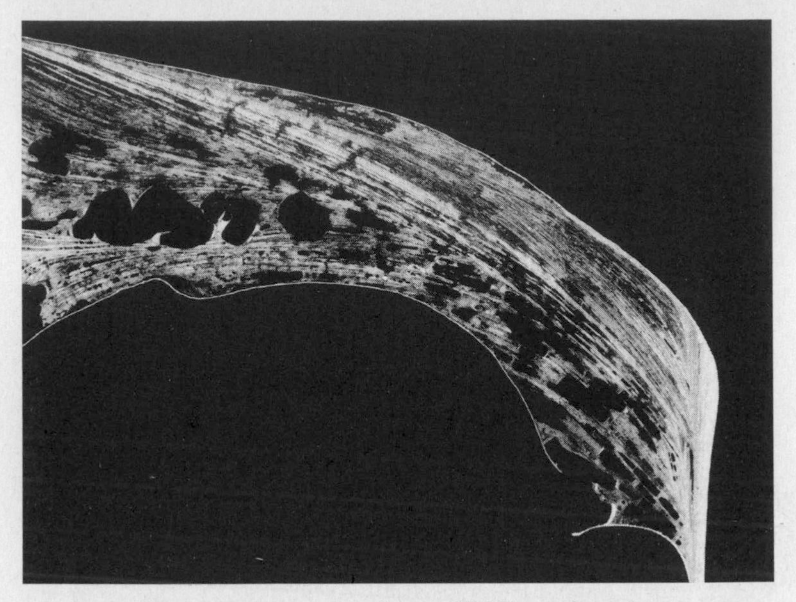

At Cape Krusenstern (shown here) Giddings found over one-hundred beach ridges containing the leavings of progressively older cultures *(Photo from Geophysical Institute, University of Alaska. Retouched for clarity.)*

oldest ridges lay farthest inland and the newest at the present shoreline, their position indicated relational age.

Further, Giddings noticed that the ages of the house pits he excavated at Choris corresponded to the ages of the ridges on which they were found. While nothing prevented a relatively younger culture from building their houses on an older beach ridge, farther from the sea, Giddings reasoned that people who hunted sea animals would find it handiest to camp close to the shore, near their boats. Hence, as one progressed inland from the sea, the ridges encountered were likely to contain the leavings of progressively more ancient people. Beach ridges,

Giddings thought, could provide a kind of horizontal stratigraphy, a new way to chart the sequence of the prehistoric cultures of Bering Strait. As he set about to find more places where beach ridges were piled up, he turned to Hopkins.

Hopkins had long been interested in ancient shorelines, and he had a good collection of aerial photos that covered all of Seward Peninsula and other places around Kotzebue Sound. He recommended that Giddings look in three places.

> I suggested Cape Espenberg, where there is a very conspicuous set of beach ridges ten or fifteen kilometers long. ... [Another was] just north of Cape Prince of Wales, where the coast swings out and a broad cluster of beach ridges confine [Lopp Lagoon]. And the third place, which had a very large sequence of beach ridges, was Cape Krusenstern. So, I suggested those places to go. During the next summer, he went to all of them. Cape Espenberg was disappointing because it was very sandy, consequently well vegetated and in part covered with large dunes and not much to see. Wales turned out to have some elevated beach ridges, and he found Denbigh material on the innermost ridge. And then everyone knows about Cape Krusenstern.

What Giddings found at Cape Krusenstern, which lies at the north entrance to Kotzebue Sound, was 114 beach ridges parallel to the shoreline and extending inland three miles from the sea. They contained a sweeping record of human habitation, older and more continuous than any beaches previously found. Every known cultural stage of prehistoric Eskimos in northern Alaska could be plotted on this remarkable full-scale graph, and there were at least two more that had not yet been recognized. Giddings' beach ridge archeology had proved a brilliant notion, and, with Hopkins' help, he continued to explore the Alaska coast looking for fossil beaches.

Hopkins followed these investigations with great interest, mainly because archeology thrilled him. He simply wanted to be a part of the exciting discoveries, like the one at Cape Denbigh, that illuminated deeper and deeper recesses in the history of human presence in the New World. But he also saw that archeology could help geologists. Giddings' dating of cultural remains permitted Hopkins to date the beach ridges within a few hundred years, to conclude that sea level then was just becoming stabilized at roughly its present level, and to begin to estimate the frequency of great storms and the rates at which the coastline had changed due to erosion and deposition.

He realized that beach ridge archeology could help geologists' attempt to verify minor sea level fluctuations thought to have occurred in the past five thousand to six thousand years, when glaciers were known to have expanded. These fluctuations had been difficult to demonstrate because sea level was frequently measured against the land's height in places where the land was subsiding. Obviously, no beach ridge dweller would dig his house into the water table. So, if house floors on a given beach at Cape Krusenstern were a foot under water (below the level of the lagoon and the sea), then either the sea level had risen, flooding the house, or the beach ridge had sunk, submerging the floor. Subsidence could be caused by regional warping or stretching of the earth's crust, or by melting of the underlying permafrost. So, if localized subsidence was the cause of a drowned house pit, it would not help date sea levels. But if a corresponding beach ridge (as identified by cultural material) at a distant place, like Cape Prince of Wales, showed the same inundation, then it more likely would be attributable to a general, worldwide change in sea level, rather than a local change due to subsidence. And an accurate history of sea level fluctuation, Hopkins figured, was the same thing as a history of the emergence and submergence of the Bering Land Bridge.

"The things that you have learned during the past summer," Hopkins wrote Giddings, "contribute tremendously to an understanding of sea level history and storm regimes. ... They hold great promise of contributing to our understanding of the precise genesis of the ridges themselves." And they set Hopkins thinking about new things: "Until I received your letter yesterday, it had never occurred to me to apply the new understanding of sea level history to an attempt to date the beginning of beach formation in western Alaska." As for Giddings, the correspondence between the two friends shows that he relied on Hopkins to suggest locations to investigate, to provide maps and aerial photos, to analyze the geology of the productive sites, to propose field strategies (such as the collection of mollusk shells), to sketch a picture of the environment thousands of years ago, to help with dating, to recommend him for funding at various agencies, and to comment generally on his emerging ideas.

Hopkins, who could not resist following his curiosity (sometimes to the exclusion of his geological research), was delighted to be involved in Giddings' discoveries. During the summer of 1959, he took time from his own fieldwork on Seward Peninsula to visit Giddings at his camp at Cape Krusenstern.

On a guided tour of the several prospects there, Hopkins, then thirty-seven years old, got a taste of what it was like to keep up with a fifty-year-old Louis Giddings when he donned his old fashioned Trapper Nelson wood and canvas packboard, pulled his ball cap down on his head, and struck out across the tundra.

> The first time I visited, we covered the whole of Cape Krusenstern. Cape Krusenstern is very, very large. The beach ridge complex itself is probably about three miles wide and tens of miles long. So we hiked a complete transect across the beach ridges near his camp. ... Then we got into an outboard and went to the inner [landward] edge of the lagoon because Louis knew where there were some shells weathering out. ... Then he wanted to take me up to see the Palisades site. So we climbed the hillside to see Palisades I and II. Then we came down, and then we hiked over to some early Thule houses, which had been burned with the occupants in them. Perhaps we didn't do all this in one day. What I recall is that we walked very, very, very many miles. Louis had long legs and we were walking side by side, but I was exerting myself. Finally, after many hours, I said, would you mind if we slowed down a bit? He said, Oh, yeah. I would have liked to have slowed down long ago. I was just trying to keep up with you.

Giddings' take on the event is supported by the recollection of Paul Dayton, Giddings' nephew and field assistant, now a professor of marine ecology at the Scripps Institution of Oceanography in California: "Hopkins came by Krusenstern just briefly when I was there and all I can remember is that he walked faster than hell! We went a long ways (several miles) each day and I had to run to keep up with him."

The horizontal stratigraphy that Louis Giddings developed at Cape Krusenstern was recognized for the spectacular discovery that it was. But some archeologists questioned his conclusion that the farthest inland sites at Krusenstern, which he called Palisades II, were two thousand years older than sites on a beach ridge he called Beach 53. These were the new cultures

A characteristic shot of J. Louis Giddings, in his wood frame Trapper Nelson backpack, using a shovel as a pointer, declaiming on a bowhead whale skull, Cape Krusenstern, 1961 *(Photo by Dave Hopkins, courtesy of Dave Hopkins)*

Giddings had found, and they both contained similar and distinctive side-notched points. Since it was possible for the Beach 53 people to have also built houses farther inland at the Palisades, the question arose as to whether Giddings' dating was wrong—that really only two phases of one culture were represented. What he needed was the incontrovertible evidence of a good vertical stratigraphy that matched the beach sequence. And rattling around in the back of Louis Giddings' mind was a clue as to where to dig for it.

Hopkins (right) and crew launch a skin boat by rolling it over an inflated seal skin, Baldwin Peninsula, 1961. Others, left to right: Dan Libsourne of Point Hope; Dick Janda, geologist; Willy Goodwin, Jr. of Kotzebue *(Photo courtesy of Dave Hopkins)*

He had seen the place twenty years earlier. In 1941, the summer after his epic solo raft and kayak trip, Giddings had returned to the Kobuk River to excavate some of the house pits he'd discovered in the earlier survey. At a place called Onion Portage (for the wild onions that grew there), Giddings dug four house pits. In House 1 he found a microblade and microcores from which microblades had been struck. The only similar artifacts ever found in Alaska to that point came from the Campus site at Fairbanks, which was thought to be a very old site. The microliths seemed out of place in the fifteenth-century Onion Portage house. For twenty years, the little flints nagged at Giddings like so many stones in his boot.

Was it possible that there were more layers of artifacts beneath the floor of House 1? Could a house builder in the thirteenth century have dug into an older house depression and so heaved up to the surface some more deeply buried materials? Could this have even happened more than once, with the flints climbing up the stratigraphic rungs with each new excavation? In the summer of 1961, Giddings decided to return to the Kobuk and investigate House 1 again in the hope of verifying Cape Krusenstern's horizontal stratigraphy.

In early July, he left his crews digging at Krusenstern and flew alone to the Kobuk. He landed above Onion Portage, unfolded a rubber kayak, and set off down the river. On July 5, he reached the familiar grassy bank, profuse with wild onions and shaded with poplars beneath a birch-covered ridge. It sat on a long, narrow peninsula around which the river coursed in a wide bend. In earlier days, when the men lined their boats up the river, the women and children could cut across the portage at the base of the peninsula, shortening their trek and picking wild onions as they went. The site had been perennially occupied, because migrating caribou habitually crossed the river here in the fall. Once out in the river, the swimming caribou could be killed easily with spears from one-man bark canoes. As an additional attraction, there was a nearby source of jade, which the hunters could work into tools while they sat in camp waiting for the caribou.

Giddings found the ground thawed about a foot deep and commenced a test excavation in one of the house pits that he had excavated twenty years earlier. "For a moment I had misgivings," he wrote later, "I remembered how well we had cleaned the floor and the deeper tunnel in front and how little reason we had then to expect anything more in the frozen ground below." Nevertheless, his shovel hadn't penetrated the length of its blade before he felt it contact a scratchy material that was not gravel. He found cracked bones and charcoal at first, then, troweling carefully, uncovered "a tantalizing group of artifacts." There were obsidian end scrapers, skinning knives, bifaces, and some sort of drill-like objects. Certain that a more complete excavation was justified, Giddings paddled down the river to Krusenstern to rejoin his crew. When the work there was finished, he and his assistants piled into small boats and motored back up the Kobuk River to excavate Onion Portage.

What Giddings and his crew found under the house at Onion Portage could not have been imagined. He had no sooner removed the layer of sod in three test cuts when he found in each "roughly matching one another and paralleling the surface of the ground, streaks of black, gray, and yellow earth." Digging further in one spot, he found "that there was no limit to the neatly stacked layering of old surfaces." The cultures he had found on the beach ridges at Cape Krusenstern were recognizable here, in the same sequence, but now stacked vertically, proving their relational age. He found both Denbigh materials and the same side-notched points that he had discovered at his Palisades II site. But the Palisades II artifacts were five feet deeper in the ground than the Denbigh materials, proving his assertion of Palisades' greater antiquity. The site was not only the finest example of distinct stratigraphy ever discovered in America, but it contained more than thirty culture layers extending back eighty-five hundred years.

It took a few years of roaming around Seward Peninsula for the idea to take shape in Hopkins' mind. He had a good friend in Bob Sigafoos who, following Eric Hultén, was interested in

Louis Giddings excavating at Onion Portage on the Kobuk River in 1964. A few months before his untimely death
*(Courtesy of Haffeneffer Museum, Brown University)*

reconstructing the ancient landscape on the basis of the living plants. His new friend Louis Giddings was the person who knew the most about the history of ancient humans near Bering Strait. And he himself was becoming increasingly interested in applying geology to date old beaches, old glaciers, changes in sea level, and so on.

> And it suddenly occurred to me that if we three got together we could perhaps solve—now put quotes around that—we could "solve" the problem of the Bering Land Bridge. We could show whether it existed or not, and when it existed or not.

It was a problem everyone was interested in, remembers Hopkins. "The land bridge was in the air. It had been for years."

# 8
# A SIMULTANEOUS EQUATION

"When you fly into Nome," Hopkins says, "you can see a dredge between you and the coast. That's Dredge 6. They had all these thaw pipes and they had a big crew—mostly King Islanders and other Iñupiat people from Nome—kind of jetting these thaw pipes down into the ground." The runoff from the ground thawing operation ran down a little swale where it carved out a system of gullies. "The first thing that a Quaternary geologist does when he sees something like that is walk it and look at the banks real close." Sure enough, Hopkins found a fossil walrus tusk, some fossil wood, a big collection of fossil fish bones, and fossil mollusk shells. As he happily gathered these treasures, he attracted the attention of William Oquilluk, "a very handsome, middle-aged Eskimo man with steel-gray hair. He came over mopping his forehead in the sunny afternoon, joking, 'Very hot today, all same like California.'"

The two struck up a conversation, and Hopkins mentioned that he was looking for shells. Oquilluk promptly suggested a number of other places that, Hopkins says, turned out to be "just loaded with shells." On a couple of occasions during that trip to Nome and on another, Hopkins sought out Oquilluk to learn new places where he might dig for shells, and also to

Hopkins in the field with weasel track vehicle, probably 1940s, probably Seward Peninsula *(Photo courtesy of Dana Hopkins)*

listen, over tea, to Eskimo stories that Oquilluk had been writing down in notebooks since about 1915. About sixty years into this project, the stories told by Oquilluk became the book *People of the Kauwerak*, written with the assistance of Laurel L. Bland. The story told by the shells led to a publication as well. With Oquilluk's help, Hopkins managed to re-collect samples of nearly all the mollusks that had ever been collected in the Bering Strait region. He saw that the few hours' work he'd done in the gully below Dredge 6 could form the core of a major scientific paper.

The land bridge, as an intermittent phenomenon, must have produced a traffic pattern something like that at a drawbridge. When the bridge was down, water traffic hove to while land traffic crossed in both directions. When the bridge disconnected, water traffic steamed through in both directions, while land traffic backed up on either shore. Hopkins saw it as a kind of reflexive equation. During any given historic period, the existence of a water connection between the North Pacific and the Arctic Oceans meant there was no land bridge. When there was a land connection between the continents, there was no seaway. So, if the fossil mollusk record could date the seaway, it would, in effect, date the land bridge.

With William Oquilluk's fossil deposits, Hopkins tried to understand the history of the old beaches on the Beringian coastline. In the marine sediments at Nome, he saw three distinct intervals where sea level had risen as high as, or higher than, the present. He began mapping the remnant of an old wave-cut scarp, an ancient high watermark that ran, hardly broken, for nearly a thousand miles, from the Arctic Coastal Plain in the north, to the Yukon River in Southwest Alaska. And he attempted to date, on the basis of the fossil record, the opening and closing of the land bridge during the last sixty million years.

William Oquilluk, a famous Iñupiat historian and author, guided Hopkins to fossil deposits that helped date the Bering Land Bridge *(Author: Courtesy of University of Alaska archives)*

He could see that, with the seaway open, marine creatures could migrate from the North Pacific, through Bering Strait, east across the Arctic Ocean, and into the North Atlantic. Fossils of these organisms, therefore, should be found in sedimentary deposits throughout that range. If he could date the old beach strata where the shells were found, he could date the periods when the land bridge was underwater. The giant snail *Neptunea*, for example, as Hopkins' friend F. S. MacNeil had shown, was a denizen of the Pacific basin for most of Tertiary time, the period extending back from about two million to about sixty-five million years ago. But *Neptunea* didn't show up in Atlantic sediments until the early Pleistocene, or about a million years ago. That suggested that the land bridge existed, blocking marine migration for most of Tertiary time, and then was flooded around the start of the Pleistocene, allowing *Neptunea* to migrate north and east to the Atlantic. On the other side of the equation, if the bridge existed during Tertiary time, then Tertiary strata in both Alaska and Siberia should yield an array of similar looking mammalian fossils. Trait differences should show up about a million years ago when a seaway partitioned Beringian populations and allowed each group to evolve separately.

As Hopkins began learning the field of molluskan paleontology, he saw that it was a mess. "If you read the literature, we had mammoths charging across the land bridge at just the same time that the big snails, *Neptunea*, were swimming through Bering Strait." Fortunately, he had two friends at the University of California at Berkeley who could help. "One was Don Savage, a vertebrate paleontologist. The other was Wyatt Durham, a molluskan paleontologist and a very, very nice man. And I decided I needed to solve this simultaneous equation, and the way to do it was to take my lunch bag and go up and have lunch with them in their office and they'd tell me."

Biostratigraphers tried to reckon the date of sedimentary layers based on the age of fossils they contained. In the days before radiocarbon dating became very reliable, however, there wasn't a good way to date the fossils. The best available method used an estimation of the rate of evolutionary change in bones, teeth, and shells. Different time scales developed because mammals evolve more quickly than do mollusks (for reasons that are still being debated). "People who worked with mollusks and foraminifera had a different idea about the ages of their deposits than the people who dealt with bones," said Hopkins. In addition, the mollusks did not live in the same kind of habitat as the vertebrates. Hence, the two kinds of fossils were not found in the same places, and that inhibited a reconciliation of the two dating schemes.

"So, I sat Don Savage and Wyatt Durham down. Well, they were older than me. I didn't sit them down. I *got* them to sit down. And we discussed this problem. That developed into a loud and rancorous argument. Savage told Durham that the mollusks were very insensitive instruments for dating because they evolved so slowly. Durham said in return that the vertebrate paleontologists were bad stratigraphers, their methods were bad, and therefore their dating was just simply not to be believed. It was a complete impasse and a great disappointment," says Hopkins. "Those guys worked in the same department. Their offices were a few doors apart, and they had never had any professional conversations—social conversations, yes; professional conversations, no."

The vertebrate researchers tended to be a more pragmatic bunch and had begun working with the new potassium-argon dating technique. People like the Geological Survey's Charles Repenning were beginning to resolve discrepancies between the bones and the mollusks, with the results generally, but not always, favoring the bone dating methods. Once, when he forced the bone people (that is to say, his colleagues) to change their time designation for a span of six million years by showing them that the mollusk chronology was right, Savage publicly chided him for disloyalty to the vertebrate party line.

Hopkins, working with fragmentary data from many geographic localities and several scientific disciplines, attempted to sort things out in a paper he published in the journal *Science* in 1959. Though he acknowledged that his proposed history of the land bridge and seaway was speculative and that new discoveries like fossil mollusk collections, submarine cores, or new stratigraphy work might easily force modification of his ideas, he nonetheless ventured a chronology. He said it looked like the land bridge existed fifty-five million years ago and that it remained in existence throughout most of Tertiary time (from two to sixty-five million years ago). He thought that indirect evidence from vertebrate paleontology suggested the bridge was broken with a waterway in the middle Eocene, about fifty million years ago. Stratigraphic evidence at Nome suggested that water also submerged the bridge about a million years ago. During the last Ice Age, the Pleistocene Epoch, he thought, the land bridge had appeared and disappeared with the numerous cycles of glaciation. It was dry land during the times when glaciers were extensive, but it was flooded by rising seas when global temperatures warmed during the interglacials. Finally, around ninety-five hundred years ago, Hopkins figured, the land bridge was inundated for the last time (to date, that is).

He didn't get everything right. More recently, investigators like Louie Marincovich, with whom Hopkins has collaborated over the years, have determined that the breach of the Bering Land Bridge that Hopkins had posited for middle Eocene time did not happen. In 1999, Marincovich and his Russian colleague Andrey Gladenkov showed that fossil mollusks could firmly date what they believe to be the first opening of Bering Strait to about five million years ago. The mollusk that told the tale was, ironically, a clam. Fossilized *Astarte*, which lived in the Arctic and Atlantic Oceans, turned up in sandstone beds on the Alaska Peninsula on the Pacific side of Beringia. That meant the strait was open at the time the sandstone was deposited.

But when was that? It turned out the best way to date the sandstone was to relate diatoms (marine microfossils) found with the clams to diatoms found in well-dated deep-sea cores. This method dates the clam to 4.8 to 5.5 million years ago. When Marincovich looked at older rock on the Pacific side and found no *Astarte* or any other species that originated in the Arctic or Atlantic Oceans, he concluded that the strait was open five million years ago, but closed before that. Other researchers, including Hopkins' friend and colleague Andrei Sher, believe that the strait could have been open much earlier. Pacific organisms found on the Arctic Ocean coast of Chukotka (thus requiring a marine connection) are dated to about nine or ten million years ago. Sher thinks Marincovich and Gladenkov's work, which properly places the first opening of Bering Strait farther back in time, is a "step in the right direction, but far from the end of the story." In any event, says Marincovich, "When Dave Hopkins and others (including me) speculated on the age of the strait's first opening, "we were truly speculating based on indirect evidence." Today, scientists believe that there were at least twenty glaciations and as many interglacials during the Pleistocene. Marincovich thinks it likely that the Bering Strait seaway existed during each of those warm interglacials, and that the Bering Land Bridge connected the continents during each of the glacials. The exact number of appearances of the land bridge might not be known for a long time, he says, though he is working on answering that question.

Hopkins' paper in *Science* brought him a huge pile of the scholarly equivalent of fan mail. "Reprint requests *poured* in," he says. "More than I'd ever received before—or since, for that matter. They came not only from geologists, but also from botanists, zoologists, entomologists, ornithologists, anthropologists and, most surprising to me, from physicians and parasitologists interested in the history and biogeography of such things as fleas and syphilis! Without realizing it, I'd launched myself into a lifetime of interdisciplinary research." Also without realizing it, Hopkins was becoming the world authority on the Bering Land Bridge, contributing his own research, but also translating, brokering, and synthesizing the work of others. One spoke of the wheel, but also its hub.

# 9
# WRITING THE BIBLE

At about this time in his efforts to nudge insular and turf-bound scientists toward communicating with one another, Hopkins got a major break. He had been, as he says, "making enough noise" about the Bering Land Bridge that John Lance, representing the International Association for Quaternary Research, visited him at his office in Menlo Park. He invited Hopkins to organize an all-day symposium on the land bridge for the INQUA conference, to be held in 1965, a year and a half hence, in Boulder, Colorado. Naturally, Hopkins was delighted. Delighted "to be noticed," first of all, and delighted "to do something prestigious." Very soon, he says, "It occurred to me that this was a way to get some of these people to talk to each other—or, at least, embarrass themselves by having their disagreements in an open forum."

Because INQUA was both international and interdisciplinary, the land bridge symposium would be the premier event for a great range of interested scholars. Anyone he might approach would be pleased to accept the invitation to prepare a paper—and that certainly was not the usual case. The papers of two dozen top people, presenting new work on a single theme, held the promise of becoming an important book. Hopkins leapt at the opportunity and sent out a call for papers. When he had finished securing commitments, he had papers in the fields of geology, molluskan paleontology, vertebrate paleontology, micropaleontology, geophysics, paleomagnetics, oceanography, geochronology, botany, cytology, paleobotany, palynology (pollen studies), physical anthropology, and archeology to be given by scientists from the United States, Canada, the Soviet Union, Germany, Great Britain, and Iceland.

Hopkins was determined not to allow factions to present their views in apparent ignorance of other differing opinions and methodologies, as his friends Don Savage and Wyatt Durham had done earlier. He wanted the meetings to be a true dialogue. To set things on that course, he first asked for lengthy abstracts from the writers. Then he sent the abstracts around to the other contributors in advance of the conference. As a result, when the people arrived at the conference in September, they were ready to exchange and debate ideas, and the conference was praised for its focused discourse and as a model for scientific symposia generally.

Crowding his luck, Hopkins used his editorial role after the conference to continue to press each contributor to deal in print with his colleagues' findings, whether those findings were complementary or paradoxical. At first, several papers arrived that "sounded as though [their authors] hadn't been present at the symposium," he says. Apparently, in that Colorado rangeland locale, the scientists seldom had heard a discouraging word. Hopkins would not play along. He would simply phone them up and say, as he did to Wyatt Durham, for example, "OK you say this happened at such a time, and Repenning is saying that something else happened that required dry land at exactly that same time. And I don't want to insist that you change your mind, but I want you to acknowledge what Repenning says and explain why you differ. And I said the same thing to Repenning. And the same went on through the whole volume."

Though it was 1965 and relations with the Soviet Union were not cordial, Hopkins longed to exchange ideas with his Russian colleagues and to bring them into the community of international scientists working on the land bridge problem. He imagined the Russians as mirror-image workers, studying in a mirror-image landscape, unnecessarily separated by a political barrier. By inviting half a dozen Russian researchers to contribute papers to his book, Hopkins was building his own bridge across Bering Strait, an intellectual one that would lead to the first reciprocal scientific exchanges between Russian and American geologists and paleontologists. But it also made for a lot of extra work. He had asked the Soviet scientists to submit their papers in both Russian and English. The latter arrived in "terrible shape," he said. The scientists had little English and their institute translator had little geology. Hopkins had never had a course in Russian, but he taught himself to transliterate with the help of a dictionary. He fixed sentence-level problems in this way, but some papers needed a complete rewrite. To do that, Hopkins recruited a Russian-speaking friend to read the paper aloud while he, himself, typed, making editorial changes as he went along. "I edited all the Russians heavily," he said, "so they didn't read like Russians writing in English anymore." When Hopkins first visited Russia two years after the book was published, he was worried about the authors' reactions. "I always expect that when I meddle with people's writing that much they will be very angry with me. Instead, the Russians were extremely pleased because I'd made their work available to the outside."

Next, Hopkins lined up a publisher, Stanford University Press in Palo Alto, practically next door to the USGS's Menlo Park offices. All of this effort took time, of course, and Hopkins did have other work to do at the Geological Survey.

Hopkins upon the publication of his soon to be classic, *The Bering Land Bridge (Photo by Gene Turner, courtesy of Dana Hopkins)*

He explained to his superiors that he was organizing this symposium, that he wanted to produce a book from it, and that during the next two years he expected to be working about half time on the book. Don Eberlein, then chief of the Alaska Branch at Menlo Park, thought that was all right and sent the proposal on to Washington for approval. Eventually, a letter came back saying, essentially, "Sounds like Dave intends to go to work for Stanford Press for a couple years. It seems as though perhaps he'd better bow out of this as gracefully as he can." Hopkins was aghast. He talked it over with Eberlein, who said, "Well, you know, just do it." Some years after Hopkins just did it, one of the Survey's Washington big shots managed to get Vice President Hubert Humphrey to tour the Menlo Park offices. On that occasion, Hopkins' superiors ceremoniously presented the vice president a copy of the freshly printed *The*

*Bering Land Bridge* as an example of the sort of excellent work the Survey sponsored.

Under Hopkins' guidance, the book fit together a number of Beringian puzzle pieces. Charles Repenning, working with mammal fossils, was able to identify three, possibly four surges of immigration over the Bering Land Bridge into the New World. At the time of the first influx identified by Repenning, about twenty million years ago, fossils—or to be more precise, the evolutionary adaptations evident in the fossils and inferred to have resulted from climate changes—suggested that the land bridge was warm-temperate, humid, and forested. During the second mammalian dispersal, around the late Pliocene and early Pleistocene, Beringia appears to have been temperate, humid, and still forested. By the time of the third pulse, in the middle Pleistocene, grasslands had taken hold, along with the forests, in a temperate climate. Not until the late Pleistocene did Repenning consider the mammal record to indicate Arctic conditions, with a flora dominated by tundra, steppe, and the scrubby northern forest called taiga.

Repenning observed another interesting fact originally noted by W. D. Matthews around the turn of the nineteenth century. Though mammals migrated across the land bridge in both directions, many times more species migrated from the Old World to the New. This may have had to do with the supercontinent of Eurasia having vastly more east-to-west distance in the north temperate latitudes than does North America. Hence, discrete populations of Old World fauna could evolve separately, adapting differently to relatively similar environmental conditions over a wide area. With more varied adaptive strategies, Eurasian fauna were more likely to flourish as they dispersed across the land bridge into North America. By contrast, there was virtually no region of North America during the

Ice Ages, except unglaciated central Alaska, in which boreal fauna could evolve—all the rest of North America's northern lands being covered with glaciers.

Repenning's findings made an important contribution to the book, as they corroborated the existence of the land bridge through the fossil record of land animals and added knowledge about the changing ecology down through the Ice Ages. Still, the geologist in Hopkins craved geophysical evidence of the land bridge, and two oceanographers named Joe Creager and Dean McManus delivered it up.

The Bering and Chukchi Seas are shallow—one hundred twenty to one hundred eighty feet—and the sea floor there is mostly flat. In fact, the continental shelf underlying the Bering Sea is one of the flattest and smoothest places on the planet. Its slope, at no more than three or four inches per mile, is almost unmeasurable. North of Bering Strait, the Chukchi Sea floor extends this barely submerged plateau some distance into the Arctic Ocean. Upon both sea bottoms a layer of marine sediment has filled in and smoothed out whatever topographic relief the bedrock underneath had when it was dry land.

In their chapter in *The Bering Land Bridge*, Creager and McManus reported having found the vestige of an ancient river at the bottom of the sea. They had drilled an ocean core through the sedimentary layer over one of the filled-in valleys in the Chukchi Sea south of Cape Thompson, near Point Hope. At the bottom of their core, they brought up sediments that were "brackish-deltaic in origin." The deposit apparently marked the head of an ancient estuary formed by a river whose tributaries included today's Kobuk and Noatak Rivers of Northwest Alaska, at a time when the sea stood about one hundred twenty-five feet below its present level. Radiocarbon dating put the material at twelve thousand to fourteen thousand years old. In other words, buried beneath the flat bottom of the sea, Creager and McManus had found a Pleistocene river valley. They called it Hope Seavalley. Hopkins called it "the clincher."

Bathymetry (the topography of the sea bottom) interested Hopkins too. In the summer of 1965 he had joined a young USGS colleague named Dave Scholl and an Icelander named Thorleifur Einarsson on board the U.S. Navy ship *Charles H. Davis* to hunt for possible undersea canyons in the Bering Sea. Hopkins had roughed out a contour map of the Bering shelf from scanty data, and he and Scholl had spent many days poring over it. They wondered if some of the occasional "holes" (deep spots near the continental shelf margin) might be canyons, rather than completely enclosed depressions, and so possible remnants of ancient river valleys.

Steaming across these holes, the ship towed a sparker, which discharged electricity into the water such that its heat created a rapidly expanding bubble of superhot water vapor that sent a sound wave bouncing off the bottom and off other layers of sediment and rock beneath the bottom. Detection equipment picked up the returning echoes, and a profile of the sea floor showed up on a roll of seismograph paper. All the scientific gadgetry resided inside a windowless trailer bolted to the deck of the ship. For most of the stormy cruise, the ship pitched and rolled atop thirty- and forty-foot waves. Inside the laboratory, with no view of the horizon, Einarsson, the Icelander, was hopelessly seasick. But Hopkins, who does not get seasick, was having the time of his life. He spent nearly twenty-four hours a day in the trailer, his eyes glued to sweeping pens that profiled the sea bottom and underlying layers. "I could hardly go to bed. For the first time in my life, I was seeing these things in real time. It was like a feast to me."

Bottled up in their heaving laboratory, the men discovered that the holes had outlets. They *were* canyons. Hopkins and Scholl explored three exceptionally large and long submarine canyons in the southeast Bering Sea at the edge of the continental shelf. One of them, Bering Canyon, was, at two hundred fifty miles in length, the longest slope valley in the world. It runs along the north side of Unimak, the most easterly of the Aleutian Islands. Another, called Zhemchug Canyon, south of St. Matthew Island, was likely the world's largest slope valley volumetrically. Most of the large undersea canyons in the world have a volume of less than three hundred cubic miles. Zhemchug Canyon's volume is greater than five thousand cubic miles. Pribilof Canyon, just southeast of St. George Island, is also one of the largest and longest of the world's submarine canyons.

More particularly, the canyons did seem to be the drowned fragments of ancient river valleys. Hopkins and Scholl thought the canyons originated in the neighborhood of fifty million years ago with subsidence and down-faulting of the bedrock, before the depressions were filled in and covered with sediments. When the sea level was lower, sediment-laden glacial runoff of the great rivers of Alaska likely scoured the canyons. Hopkins and Scholl believed that Zhemchug Canyon represented the Ice Age mouth of the Yukon River. They thought the Kuskokwim River, as well as the Yukon, had at times flowed through Pribilof Canyon. And they believed Bering Canyon received its runoff from the glaciated highlands surrounding Bristol Bay and possibly from the Kuskokwim River as well. Another puzzle piece seemed to fit into place.

On the release of *The Bering Land Bridge* in 1967, reviews from around the world streamed in to the offices of Stanford University Press. Hopkins' file contains five German language reviews, three in French, others in Danish, Dutch, Russian, Swedish, and several in English (American and the Queen's). They hailed it as "an extremely important reference," "a most significant," "valuable and fascinating book," a "masterful job of editing," "remarkably cohesive" and "readable." Readable it was, especially Hopkins' writing. The book opens lyrically and memorably with these lines:

> Eighteen years ago, storm bound at Wales village, I studied the mist smoking over a turbulent Bering Strait and wondered who, on this violent day, might be shouldering the wind on the Asian shore to share my search for traces of the past. Near me rose a peaty mound, the midden left by generation upon generation of Eskimos dwelling at the western tip of North America; behind me rose Cape Mountain, scarred by ancient glaciers, carved by ancient waves. Perhaps someone was at that moment sheltering his Cyrillic notes from the mist as he huddled on a terrace on East Cape, at the eastern tip of Siberia—or in an Eskimo burial ground at Uelen, Siberia's easternmost village.

Hopkins dedicated the book to his two Beringian exemplars, Eric Hultén and Louis Giddings.

# 10

# THE PRODUCTIVITY PARADOX

In 1916, a Swedish botanist mucking around in some old Scandinavian bogs discovered that fossil pollen grains showed up in the peat of prehistoric swamps. Under magnification, Lennart von Post could see their distinctive shapes and surface patterns. They looked like spiny harbor mines or pockmarked asteroids, others like soccer balls, bathyspheres, space capsules, or capsules of ibuprofen. By their shapes, von Post could identify the kinds of plants that produced them.

Lots of plants, especially wind-pollinated ones, annually produce virtual dust storms of pollen. A single conifer can produce twenty-one billion pollen grains each year. The winds carry them aloft and mix them with other pollen to descend on the landscape in a kind of pollen rain. Some of this fallout lands on ponds and lakes, or makes its way there via streams. Eventually, the pollen sifts down to the bottom, settling in strata along with other organic matter and dust. The grains have a tough, decay-resistant shell to start with, but when they are submerged or waterlogged, hence in a low-oxygen environment, they stand a good chance of being preserved for thousands of years.

To von Post, the pollen strata offered a peephole on the past. He could watch the changes in the plant life of Northern Europe, as the Ice Age ended and the glaciers melted away. In the changing ratios of pollen grains, he saw the dominant tundra plants yielding to birch trees and the birches suffering the invasion of oaks until a mixed oak forest prevailed. Because plants reflect the climate in which they grow, and because plant matter is organic and can be radiocarbon dated, fossil pollen could identify and date ancient plant cover. Pollen became a useful tool in reconstructing the prehistoric landscape and climate.

Back in the mid-1950s, when Hopkins was camped at Imuruk Lake on the Seward Peninsula, he was reminded of the science of palynology. His major professor at Harvard, Kirk Bryan, now considered by many to be the father of Quaternary geology, was not a typical geologist of his day. An interdisciplinary thinker, Bryan encouraged his students to bring multiple lines of evidence to bear on their problems. He passed on to Hopkins what he was hearing about pollen science, suggesting that it might be both a way to date sedimentary layers and a useful tool in reconstructing the ancient history of a region's vegetative cover. Hopkins thought Imuruk Lake must be a very old lake and that it should have a very long pollen record. So he wrote to the handful of people he knew who did pollen coring suggesting the lake's possibilities. One by one, each turned him down. Hopkins says that researchers were used to doing fieldwork near the road system and were not much attracted to Imuruk Lake, five hundred roadless miles west of Fairbanks (itself not an easy place to get to). Furthermore, Imuruk Lake wasn't just a long way from grocery stores, showers, and Laundromats. It was truly wild: desolate, windy, cold, wet, teeming with mosquitoes, gnats, and bears.

"So, crafty old Dave wrote this article," Hopkins says with a chuckle, "The History of Imuruk Lake.'" The sole purpose of the piece, he says, was to build toward a punch line: that a major contribution to the scientific understanding of Beringia lay in the unexplored sediments of Imuruk Lake. Immediately after its publication in the *Geological Society of America Bulletin* in 1959, the letters began arriving. And sure enough the next year a Ph.D. student from Yale named Paul Colinvaux came to Alaska to attempt to core the sediments of Imuruk Lake.

Colinvaux found conditions at Imuruk Lake approximately as advertised. Unremitting winds and choppy water made drilling in the deep lake's bottom difficult. Impossible, actually. He had to abandon his first attempt and consider a try in winter from the stable platform of the frozen lake surface. Gamely, he returned for what was Arctic Alaska's first winter lake-coring project. His initiative was rewarded. The pollen core he took from Imuruk Lake permitted the reconstruction of vegetation changes at the eastern edge of the Bering Land Bridge over at least the previous one hundred fifty thousand years. It was, Hopkins felt, probably the most remarkable pollen record ever made in Beringia.

From this start, Paul Colinvaux became the dean of a school of thought that recreates the environment of the last land bridge as an unproductive place, a windy and forsaken landscape of sparse tundra, "a dusty plain stretching to the horizon, vegetated between the bare patches with a low mat of sedges and grasses looking like a drier version of the modern Arctic plain." In this vision, the animal population was minimal, mainly a few rodent species. The few large animals that may have wandered through were itinerants ranging out from the main herds that occupied the forested areas of the adjacent continental landmasses. For years, most scholars accepted this view of Beringia, buttressed by the Imuruk Lake core. But by the mid-1960s, a completely contradictory theory began to gain ground.

About the time that Hopkins was bobbing around on the Bering Sea, surveying submarine canyons, a student at the University of Alaska named John Matthews was taking up the study of fossil insects in the Pleistocene mucks of Alaska. Hopkins remembers Matthews approaching him at a conference. "He said he had a good Wisconsin [glacial stage] fauna from various exposures around Fairbanks, and he was interested in carrying the record further back, and did I have any special place to suggest. I suggested Cape Deceit on Kotzebue Sound near the village of Deering, on the north shore of Seward Peninsula. I had reason to think that Cape Deceit had a record that went at least back through the next to last glaciation, the Illinoian. I had no idea that it would go back possibly into the Pliocene. So the next summer, which was '66, I was camped in Deering, and Dale Guthrie and John Matthews appeared and set up a tent beside the shack my party was living in. They started digging up Cape Deceit, which turned out to be one of the most important contributions ever to Beringian paleoecology."

At Cape Deceit, Guthrie, a professor at the University of Alaska Fairbanks, and Matthews, his graduate student, found a vertically exposed face of earth about thirty feet high and running intermittently along the beach for about eight hundred feet. The stratified layers of exposed soil showed bands of gray and dark olive silts, peaty material, woody zones, gravel, sand,

and ice wedges above a pale yellow form of limestone. They found fossil teeth of large mammals such as elk, caribou, horse, wapiti, and wolf, as well as of the most primitive ancestors of the small mammal lineages of voles, lemmings, and pikas that populate the Arctic tundra today. One collared lemming fossil represented a completely new genus and species. And the oldest sedimentary layer contained the earliest North American record of several species, and the only North American record of the Eurasian rodent, *Pliomys*, a seed eater that presumably occupied the ecological niche now filled by the red-backed vole. When Charles Repenning reviewed the discovery, he said they were "Siberian fauna ... on the wrong side of Bering Strait." The animals dated to 1.8 to 2.5 million years ago, predating the Pleistocene.

In addition to the mammal remains, Matthews and Guthrie found fossil pollen, plant fragments, and the body parts of assorted insects. Plant fossils included seeds, cones, and leaves of white spruce and tamarack, revealing that the tree line had at least twice been as far west as Cape Deceit. To obtain insect parts, the investigators first sieved the dirt with screens. Submersing the screened material in water allowed the researchers to skim off body parts, sort them under a microscope, and glue them to slides. They collected peat samples in blocks, because peat frequently contained the best preserved insect remains. Like opening a carefully packed Christmas box, the lab workers teased apart chunks of peat to remove entomological gifts as prized as tissue-wrapped pears from Harry & David. They removed any fragments of leafhopper, beetle, or weevil and mounted them on a macrofossil slide for identification. This could be an indecorous business. Certain species of ground beetle of the subgenus *Cryobius*, for example, can be reliably identified only by careful examination of the male genitalia.

The upshot of Guthrie and Matthews' multifaceted analysis, as well as much additional work by Matthews, was a picture of the evolution of the tundra ecosystem at Deering, extending back through the whole of the Pleistocene and beyond. It showed that, during the early Pleistocene, the tundra at Deering was dry and scantily vegetated. By the middle Pleistocene, however, it was becoming grassier, culminating in steppelike tundra by the last glaciation. With cycles of warmer weather, the tree line had moved west, receding to interior regions again with cooling trends. Insects, it seemed, had done little in situ evolving. Meanwhile, the small mammal record showed evolutionary changes (presumably in response to changing tundra conditions) over the last four hundred thousand to nine hundred thousand years.

Another result of this work was the assigning of the name *Predicrostonyx hopkinsi* to a newly discovered beast, an extinct denizen of Beringia. *Predicrostonyx* for its likely ancestral relationship to *Dicrostonyx*, the present-day collared lemming, and *hopkinsi* for Hopkins, who had suggested Cape Deceit as a good place to look for fossils.

The Cape Deceit exposure shed its fossils for Guthrie and Matthews just thirty-five miles from Imuruk Lake, where Hopkins had enticed Colinvaux to lift his pollen core. But if their field camps were in the same neighborhood, Paul Colinvaux and Dale Guthrie's camps of learned opinion were not. Their disagreements over the reconstruction of the ecology of Beringia during the last Ice Age has blossomed into what is no doubt the longest running controversy in the annals of Beringian scholarship, maybe in all of Arctic paleontology.

The smoldering differences erupted with the publication of Hopkins' second land bridge book in 1982.

With his first book, *The Bering Land Bridge*, Hopkins and colleagues had firmly established that the land bridge must have existed. For one thing, sea level had fluctuated enough to expose the shallow continental shelf. For another, the submerged meanders of former river channels indicated they were once part of a terrestrial drainage system. And, unless it was Noah's work, animal exchanges between Asia and North America simply required a land connection. At that point, says Hopkins, "the interesting question became: to what extent could we reconstruct ancient environments on or near the land bridge? And, more particularly, to what extent could we reconstruct the environment of the most recent land bridge, the land connection that existed during some, perhaps all, of the Wisconsin cold period?" If scholars could pull together a picture of the paleoecology, it would permit a deeper look into the history of the Americas and, not least, at the story of the first human entry into the New World.

Shortly after he finished *The Bering Land Bridge*, Hopkins remembers attending a meeting in Arizona where John Matthews and Charlie Schweger were attending graduate school. Matthews had already done his work with Dale Guthrie at Cape Deceit, and Schweger was spending summers at Gidding's find at Onion Portage, also in northwest Alaska. "Those two guys are very aggressive and somehow they got hold of a list of the people who were invited to this National Academy of Sciences Polar Research Board meeting and found out I was there." Schweger and Matthews asked Hopkins if he would mind talking to them. "I said sure, so they came out to my motel with a six-pack—or maybe a bottle of Old Crow—

and we sat around and talked all evening. It was a very exciting evening and, you know, it was partly the land bridge book that had caught fire with them." Hopkins suggested Schweger investigate old looking strata exposed along Epiguruk Bluff on the Kobuk River, one bend above Onion Portage. The pollen analysis Schweger did there later became the basis of his Ph.D. dissertation at the University of Alberta.

Before the bottles were empty that night, Hopkins and the two dedicated students resolved to form a Beringian study group. "Study group" is too grand a name, says Hopkins, but the three did stay in touch over the next several years. They were a nucleus with potential, and there came a point in the early 1970s when they felt that enough new knowledge had been developed that it was possible to describe in far greater detail what the Beringian landscape looked like. "We decided that we ought to organize some big meeting," says Hopkins. "The first symposium had been so successful that we ought to organize another. Because, by this time we were 'we.'"

It took a few more years for the pieces to fall into place. During the summer of 1976, Hopkins traveled to a castle in the Austrian Alps to attend a conference on early man in America, sponsored by the Wenner Gren Foundation. A few months later, he found himself again at a meeting in Arizona, in a session devoted to Beringian questions. Again, John Matthews and Charlie Schweger were there. The attendees visited a mammoth kill site, and, on the return bus ride, Hopkins' seatmate asked how his summer was going. "Charlie and John were in the back of the bus. We had just been to a mammoth site. And I was sitting telling what I'd been doing that summer—about the glorious experience I had at the Burg Wartenstein conference and what a great place it was to have a meeting and how much you could put together at a meeting.

All of a sudden I jumped up and said, 'Excuse me,' and ran back to John and Charlie and said, 'Hey, I know where we can have our Beringian conference!' We got to Tucson—the meeting was over—we went out and drank beer at a Mexican restaurant and pretty much organized our own Burg Wartenstein conference that night." If it seemed less than auspicious to sit in the Arizona desert, under the influence of a Mexican beer, to brainstorm a visit to a European castle to solve an Arctic mystery, it didn't get in their way.

The 1979 conference produced the 1982 book *The Paleoecology of Beringia*, coauthored by Hopkins and his young colleagues Matthews, Schweger, and Steven B. Young. Schweger looked at the pollen data taken from cutbanks of rivers in Alaska and the Yukon Territory and was led to reject any idea of a "uniform vegetative cover that can easily be summarized as steppe-tundra." Instead, he saw a more complex system of vegetative zones where the plant composition was influenced by elevation and the availability of surface water. The floodplains of the late Wisconsin, Schweger said, featured a variety of open and aquatic habitats dominated by willow and sedge. Moving higher in elevation, tundra and grasslands occupied the benches, and a sparse, dry tundra climbed the foothills, playing out on the slopes of mountains. Matthews, who looked not only at pollen, but at plant and insect fossils, thought the data "rule out a monolithic Arctic steppe ... but they are still compatible with an environment containing a vegetational mosaic that included extensive tracts of steppe."

Paul Colinvaux was not on the list of invitees to the Burg Wartenstein conference, much to his consternation. The number of participants had been kept small due to accommodations limits, and another palynologist, James Ritchie, was there who agreed with Colinvaux that Beringia was vegetatively impoverished. Ritchie concluded that the landscape during the last glacial period had been only spottily covered with herbaceous tundra in the uplands and sedge-grass meadows in the low areas. Like Colinvaux, he sees the vegetative mix as able to support primarily rodents. As for the notion of a complex community of large mammals sustained by a productive grassland, Ritchie and his coauthor Les Cwynar wrote, "we suggest that the 'Arctic-steppe biome' never existed" in Alaska or the Yukon during the last twenty-five thousand years. In fact, while they were inclined to believe that diverse ungulate (hoofed animals, including mammoth) populations probably roamed Beringia during the warmer (interstadial) periods of the last Ice Age, they questioned whether during the colder times, when the land bridge was at its broadest, such herds were present at all.

Palynologists generally concede that the odd mammoth and bison ventured out onto the land bridge from adjacent forested areas by browsing along the more productive river valleys. They note the paucity of late Pleistocene windblown pollen showing up in lake sediment cores, as well as the lack of trees or even good-sized shrubs. Cwynar and Ritchie, like Colinvaux, insist that their data describe a generally inhospitable and nutritionally unproductive place: dusty, dry, windy, barren, and cold. In short, a polar desert.

In his contribution to the conference and book, vertebrate paleontologist Dale Guthrie offered, among other arguments, a bit of logic as concrete as an eight-foot mammoth tusk dripping mud on a pollen counter's desk: The fossilized remains of the beasts turn up in the New World. The large animals *must* have crossed the land bridge. And they couldn't have done it without eating along the way.

Paintings of Ice Age mammals by George Teichmann: "Scimitar Cat and Saiga Antelope" (top) and "Lions and Mammoths" *(Courtesy of Department of Tourism and Culture, Government of Yukon, Canada)*

As Guthrie and Matthews interpret their data, Beringia was an extension of a vanished ecological array, not precisely like any modern analog. It spread from today's Yukon Territory across Alaska and Asia to the Atlantic coast of Europe—a high latitude grassland nearly encircling the globe. It was a unique and productive ecosystem, says Guthrie, supporting large populations of many species, as well as the men who hunted them. The vegetation—nutritious and dominated by grass and sedge—covered a firmer substrate than today's mushy, wet tundra. He paints a picture of a tundra-steppe that functioned ecologically more like an African savanna than like contemporary Arctic tundra. And, like the highly productive Serengeti Plains of East Africa, it was home, he says, to great aggregations of animals. More outsized and fantastic even than their modern African counterparts, the Pleistocene megafauna included woolly mammoth, woolly rhino, large-horned bison, giant ground sloth, Pleistocene horses, muskoxen, camel, Dall sheep, caribou, broad-fronted moose, elk, saiga antelope, and giant beaver. And pursuing these were the saber-toothed cats, steppe lions, giant short-faced bears, grizzly bears, and wolves.

Hence, two seemingly irreconcilable facts seemed to emerge from the research: The land bridge seems to have supported sparse vegetation, *and* it seems to have fed a large diversity of grazing animals. It was a paradox—the "productivity paradox," as it came to be called.

# 11
# MAMMOTH FAUNA

Since Alaska's gold rush days of a century ago, gold miners have been digging through deposits of silt that overlie gold-bearing gravels. As they stripped the overburden, or muck, with hydraulic hoses, they washed out hundreds of thousands of Pleistocene mammal fossils. To date the old bones, it is important to examine the specific layer of earth from which they came. Unfortunately, most bones are picked up at the bottom of a thawing face, having fallen out of their stratigraphic context. Every part of Alaska that was unglaciated during the last Ice Age has produced fossils of large mammals, especially bison, horse, and mammoth. Guthrie points out that the frequency of these finds seems to correlate with the degree of mining activity, suggesting that the more we have dug, the more we have found. The fossils date to as far back as radiocarbon dating can take us, about forty thousand years, well beyond the last glacial maximum.

The mammoth fauna, as the Russians call the large-mammal aggregations, seem to have roamed all over Beringia throughout the entire duration of the last glaciation. But in what concentrations? It's hard to say. What is known, according to Guthrie, is that the three key species—bison, horse, and mammoth—made up most of the mammalian biomass on the last land bridge. And they were gregarious. Where there was one horse or bison, there was likely a herd, small or large. Judging from the habits of modern elephants, mammoth probably collected in matriarchal nursery herds of at least six to eight cows and calves, with the bulls being more solitary. A concentration of animals into herds implies a concentration of feed as well. Areas of adequate forage had to be near enough to one another that the animals could move between them without the energy cost of travel exceeding the energy value of the nutrition. As to the character of that fodder, Colinvaux suggests that the few large animals that walked the land bridge were browsers (shrub eaters), sustaining themselves on the tundra plants of a polar desert—the lichen and miniature herbs and shrubs that the pollen analysts say were there. But Guthrie notes that several clues indicate that bison, horse, and mammoth were not browsers, but grazers, grass eaters.

In the Kolyma region of Siberia, in 1900, word began to spread that a great "devil creature" could be seen sitting in the mud of an eroding stream bank on the Berezovka River. Fortunately, word spread all the way to Moscow and reached the Imperial Academy of Sciences. With the spring thaw, the academy launched an expedition. After a journey of more than four months into eastern Siberia, the biologists reached the mammoth in late September. According to the local Lamut people, the creature's head had emerged from the thawing permafrost two years earlier. Dogs and wolves had been at it, and a hunter had liberated the tusks. Still, much of the carcass was buried in the icy mud, and the frozen meat was so well preserved it looked edible. The circumspect scientists passed up their chance to sample a Pleistocene dish that had been out of season for ten thousand years. Instead, they gave their dogs the honor without ill effect. As for the mammoth's last meal, it had been grasses, along with two sedges, a mint, and the pods and beans of a leguminous plant. From between the beast's great, stony teeth, the Russians pried flowers identified as buttercups.

In the 1970s, Siberian gold miners, working thirty feet underground near the Selerikan River, found it handy to hang a lantern from a knobby protuberance jutting from the ceiling of their tunnel. Eventually, somebody took a closer look at the thing and discovered that it was the hind leg of an apparently ancient horse, with the rest of the animal still frozen in the earth above. The miners notified members of the Siberian Academy of Sciences who agreed that a Pleistocene horse mummy might be put to better use than as a lantern peg. The beautifully preserved specimen proved to be a stallion with a two-inch-thick coat. It was a light yellowish color underneath and coffee brown above, like a modern bay, but with a black mane and a dark streak running all the way down its spine to a black tail. The horse likely became bemired thirty-seven thousand years ago, probably in late autumn, judging by the thick winter coat, the fat deposits around the heart, and the mature seeds and pollen in his full gastrointestinal tract. Well-preserved stomach contents contained more than ninety percent herbaceous material, nearly all of which was grasses. Of the pollen, researchers found it to be almost entirely from graminoids (sedges and grasses) with grasses twice as plentiful as sedges. The Selerikan horse, like the Berezovka mammoth, was a grazer.

Yet another Siberian gold miner stripping silty overburden in the next river valley to the east in 1977, exposed a completely intact baby mammoth. Dima, as the Russians called him, probably was only four months of age when he died ten thousand to forty thousand years ago (wood found near the animal gives the later date; the skin gives the older one). He likely froze shortly after being trapped in a sinkhole of organic-rich, saturated silt. In open air, freeze-drying will occur as an object loses moisture by sublimation, where ice vaporizes without first liquefying. Alaskan pioneer women knew about this and sometimes hung wet clothes outside to dry in extremely cold temperatures. Dale Guthrie points out that a similar but not identical process happens with frozen material that is not exposed to air. Moisture migrates to the surface where it collects as ice. In this way, a wrapped piece of meat may become encased in ice after many months in the freezer. With Dima, this drying or mummification process worked in textbook fashion and resulted in perhaps the best-preserved specimen of a large animal ever found in the North.

Pollen found around Dima's body suggested to Russian botanists that he lived in a dry, steppe tundra landscape where trees grew in the river valleys. Dima's gastrointestinal tract was empty, likely because he starved over several days of entrapment. But the researchers found gut material in his colon, where pollen percentages showed sixty-seven percent grasses, suggesting a vegetative mix similar to modern cold mountain steppe regions.

As Hopkins and coauthors sorted out the ecological picture of Beringia in the synopsis of their book, they tended toward a scenario that included the steppe theory. Today, East and West Beringia are home to vast expanses dominated by sedge marsh, sedge-tussock tundra, dwarf shrub lands, and forests. But forty millennia ago, the vegetative mix may have been quite different. It may have favored extensive meadows and steppe tundra in the uplands, and shrub thickets in the moister areas such as flood plains and those shaded pockets where snow beds might persist. There may have been some open woodland in the hills, and lines of trees along the watercourses. Certainly, as the climate shifted to the very cold and dry period of the late Wisconsin of twenty thousand years ago, the vegetation array became more impoverished. But it would have been a diminished version of the vegetative picture found during the earlier, warmer ecosystem of the interstadial, not a richer version of today's tundra plants. So plant cover during the last land bridge was sparse, according to Hopkins' notions. But a mix of graminoid (grass-type) plants and a variety of herbs still covered much of Beringia. And grasses, which are more digestible, can account for greater animal biomass than an equivalent amount of tundra. True polar desert was probably limited to the high Arctic, due to the infrequent penetration of moist air masses from the south.

With respect to animal migrations across the land bridge, climate and terrain acted together as a kind of cold filter controlling which species could move between the continents. Insect fauna from this period tend to be those that favored dry substrates and a treeless landscape. Notable among these is the dung beetle, which exists in association with ungulates. Fossils of mammals, Hopkins and colleagues concluded, clearly establish the presence in parts of Beringia of mammoth, bison, horse, caribou, mountain sheep, and saiga, as well as muskox, not just during the warmer interstadial, but during the coldest period also. The various ungulates may have grazed the same feed patch, but in a complementary way. A bison could feed where a horse had been, for instance, because the horse was a stem clipper and left a lot of stalk standing. The bison grabbed grass with its tongue, tearing it some inches above the base and leaving the lip feeders (saiga and mountain sheep) to mow down the stubble.

Things changed again, and radically, about fourteen thousand years ago. The vast ice sheets melted away, and sea level rose, finally lapping over the land bridge. Rapid spring melting of the winter's snow pack brought roaring gully washouts and floods. Lush vegetation grew during the sunny summers, and cottonwood trees advanced a hundred miles beyond their present range. At the same time, the great mammals of the land bridge lumbered into the mists, never to be seen again. Wooly mammoth disappeared soon after fourteen thousand years ago, followed by the Pleistocene horse a thousand years later, and bison a couple of thousand years after that.

Reviewers of *Paleoecology of Beringia* found its "integrative editorial work" to be "exceptional," and "required reading" for scientists in the field. The summary chapter written by Hopkins, "the acknowledged dean of Beringian studies," was said to be "like his earlier syntheses, the 'state of the art' statement on the overall characteristics of Beringia." Scholars took to calling Hopkins' latest book The New Testament and his earlier one The Old Testament. Paul Colinvaux, however, withheld his imprimatur. Among Hopkins disciples, he was the schismatic, finding much of which to disapprove. Writing in the *Quarterly Review of Archeology*, he scoffed at the book's "assumption of a land bridge fit for big game animals and human heroes to live in." "They talk of a 'mammoth-steppe,'" he wrote, as a place where many animals lived "in productive harmony as in the game herds of modern East Africa." "This conception of the Bering Land Bridge is contrary to the evidence," said Colinvaux, and "likely to perpetuate myths about the land bridge which ought to be decently buried."

Rejecting the vegetation picture offered by coauthor Young, Colinvaux vouchsafed that it was "a simple denial of the pollen data more proper to speculations of the 1930s than an assessment of modern evidence." No gentler in reaction to Guthrie's ideas, Colinvaux found it inconceivable that "virtually all the animals ever found associated with Beringia might be put together to form a complex grazing ecosystem." "Few scientists," he said, "can be expected to take this seriously."

Going beyond a critique of the book, Colinvaux offered his own interpretation of the data. He pointed out that some investigators, including Hopkins himself, had recognized geologic evidence supportive of the palynologists' view that the land bridge was largely bare. Hopkins and others had compiled a map showing fossil sand dunes from the far north to the Pribilof Islands, many apparently contemporary with the glacial maximum. The study showed that winds deposited loess (windblown silt) at this time, and that suggested the presence of bare ground and dry, windy conditions.

Addressing himself to the inescapable fact of mammoth bones turning up in Beringia, Colinvaux postulated that mammoth "undertaking long seasonal migrations, particularly on the Siberian side, could journey in winter to more productive vegetation, even to a forest ecotone." Because the stomach contents of frozen mammoth mummies contained summer vegetation, Colinvaux concluded, "It seems likely the animals migrated well to the south for winter feeding."

Guthrie responded, though without derision, in the same journal some months later. There were problems with the palynologists' basic approach to analyzing their data, he said. It was true that overall pollen influx, as they called the annual accumulation of grains, was low during the glacial maximum as compared to the current epoch, the Holocene. But, as Guthrie pointed out, trees show up in Holocene pollen counts. And it is the habit of northern trees to produce blizzards of pollen. Trees were absent, or nearly so, from the land bridge in glacial times, and that fact better explains why the total pollen production was much lower. So, low pollen counts during the Pleistocene do not necessarily mean that the vegetation was correspondingly impoverished during those times. What Guthrie suggested—and went on to do—was factor out the tree pollen and compare the pollen production from herbs (non-woody plants).

It turns out that herb pollen production, as a percentage of total pollen production, was actually greater during the Ice Ages than during the Holocene—several times greater. If the assumption is correct that the amount of pollen correlates with the volume of vegetation, said Guthrie, then the volume of herbaceous vegetation at the time of the land bridge must have been much greater than it is today. He also noted that most herbaceous plants in the north are not large pollen producers and that grasses, in response to grazing, can easily shift from sexual reproduction (via pollen) to vegetative reproduction (via creeping stems). Besides, many plants deliver pollen through the agency of insects, rather than wind, and are therefore invisible in the pollen record. With this evidence and reasoning, Guthrie discounted the idea that the low pollen influx during the glacial period could be accounted for only by a polar desert or barren tundra.

Next, the matter of the mammoths. To Colinvaux's suggestion that the harsh environment could not have supported the full array of "mammoth fauna," Guthrie presented lists of bones directly dated to the time in question. He showed that the main species roamed Alaska during the entire span of time measurable by radiocarbon dating. As for the idea that mammoth must have migrated far to the south seasonally, Guthrie said it was not possible that frozen mammoth mummies found in the north had "southern" grasses in their gut. He noted that proboscidians have a "gut transit time" on the order of twelve hours. Moreover, migration didn't square with the energy budget. Walking for the mammoths—swinging their heavy, distally weighted legs—required more energy than was the case with the more gracile ungulates such as caribou. Mammoths may have wandered nomadically, but they needed their feed to be near enough at hand (or trunk) that it didn't cost substantial energy to reach it. Beyond that, there was the fact that thousands of miles of glaciers stood between a mammoth in Alaska and southern forage. If a mammoth could get across the glaciers (without eating, apparently), why would it leave a richly productive zone each summer to migrate across ice to a polar desert?

Guthrie had more arguments to fortify his reconstruction of Beringia. Hoof morphology of the fossil ungulates, for instance, indicated they lived on firm, dry ground suitable for running. For most ungulates, running was a principal defense against predators. Today's wet tundra is so boggy and yielding that running is nearly impossible without special foot adaptations, like a split hoof that splays apart to distribute the load over more surface area or a leg that lifts vertically out of the mud. The presence of saiga, horse, bison, and mammoth, which did not have these adaptations to any substantial degree, suggested a firm substrate where grasses might do well.

The fact that the Pleistocene fauna were giants and carried great horns and antlers and tusks also offered clues. Where habitat is marginal, animals tend to develop small body size, and the appendages not directly associated with survival tend toward the diminutive. Land bridge mammals, by contrast, displayed great size and elaborate headgear. They seemed to be taking full advantage of plentiful and high-quality summer feed.

In the same journal, two issues later, Colinvaux launched a second salvo at what he called Guthrie's rejection of "all the arguments of every palynologist who has ever worked in Alaska" and his vision of a "mighty steppe homeland of the mammoths." He again cited geophysical evidence to describe the growing conditions on the land bridge: "frozen ground; clouds of loess; katabatic [downward blowing] winds from glaciers; desperate long winters; short summers, in places drier or warmer than now; these were the conditions for plant life in which the ancient tundras were put together." Even though the existence of the animals can be proven by directly dated fossil remains, while vegetation is only inferred from recovered pollen, Colinvaux insisted that more would be learned "by asking how animals, even if only a few, could adapt to the Arctic tundras of the place than in requiring the place to adapt to the animals."

That concluded the exchange in *Quarterly Review of Archeology*, but the colloquy has continued, at intervals, throughout the years since. Guthrie restated and amplified his arguments in a 1990 book called *Frozen Fauna of the Mammoth Steppe*. By then, he had even picked out the tiny plant fragments that lodged in the central recesses of the teeth of Pleistocene ungulates. Under a microscope, specialists can identify the plant family from which the masticated plant matter came. In fossil bison, horse, and woolly rhino teeth, Guthrie found that grasses dominated by a wide margin.

In 1996, a paleoecologist named Scott Elias and coworkers published a paper in the journal *Nature* based on Bering and Chukchi Sea cores collected decades earlier by Lawrence Phillips of the U.S. Geological Survey. Elias found pollen and other organic remains in peat layers dating to the land bridge period. From this evidence, he concluded that the lower, now-submerged areas of the land bridge supported a wet shrub tundra vegetation and that no evidence suggested steppe tundra. Paul Colinvaux wrote a "gotcha" piece in the same issue, declaring that Elias's new data had finally settled the issue: "Beringia was tundra, not steppe."

The long-running controversy, which started when Hopkins guided both Colinvaux and Guthrie to remarkable discoveries on Seward Peninsula, circled back to Hopkins when he turned up yet another spectacular find.

# 12

# SOIL FROM MAARS

Hopkins first saw the evidence in 1966, but it was years before its meaning resolved itself in his mind. He had been working on northern Seward Peninsula, based out of Deering, an Eskimo village of fewer than a dozen families. Deering had no electricity, and the abandoned shack Hopkins occupied had only a dirt floor. He was looking into the marine geology of offshore gold placers when he thought it wise to pay some attention to placers on the adjacent land. He chartered a Supercub on floats from a fellow named Buck Maxon, who engaged John Cross to fly it. By then, Cross had been flying Hopkins around Seward Peninsula for twenty years. "Buck let him fly it out of love for John," says Hopkins, because Cross was by then in his seventies. He was still a good pilot, though, even sleeping in a tent beside the plane (people along the coast didn't consider it stealing to liberate a little gas).

One morning, Hopkins decided to investigate the mouth of the Goodhope River in Goodhope Bay, and Cross flew him over there. Rather than landing, though, Cross flew in circles for some time. "I was starting to see a barrel here, a stump there," says Hopkins. "Pretty soon I said, 'Maybe we'd better not land here.' John said, 'That's what I was hoping you'd say.'" A little later, on the twenty-fifth of July, Hopkins and Cross tried another spot, Devil Mountain Lakes just south of

Cape Espenberg. Since the late 1940s, when the Navy took the first aerial photos of the area, Hopkins had been curious about the strange round lakes. There were five of them in a row, one a double, interlocking lake, like a figure eight. He thought they looked like craters from a meteor that had fractured before impact. In 1948, he was able to fly over Devil Mountain Lakes, the double lake, and could see the steeply sloping walls indicative of craters. But now, in 1966, when he climbed out of the Supercub onto its beach and saw that it was strewn with bullet-sized pieces of volcanic ejecta, he knew at once that the craters were the result of volcanic explosions. They were maars.

A maar is a volcano that may erupt explosively, directly from a level plain. It usually fills with water to become a more or less circular lake. Though the average diameter of a maar is just seven hundred fifty yards, South Devil Mountain Lake is two miles across, and North Devil Mountain Lake is three miles across. They are believed to be the largest maars in the world and among the northernmost volcanoes in North America.

Thousands of years ago, according to Hopkins' reconstruction, molten rock, perhaps thirty miles below the surface of the northern Seward Peninsula and under great pressure, began to work its way upward through a weakness or fracture in the overlying mantle. Eventually, the rising basaltic magma reached a thick and unusually porous layer of rock, saturated with ground water. Ground water became ground steam, and pressures began to build. A lid of permafrost—perhaps more than three hundred feet thick—held back the imminent explosion like a champagne cork whose wire cage has been removed—that is to say, momentarily. At the instant that steam pressure exceeded the tensile strength of a three-hundred-foot-thick frozen slab, the earth above heaved itself into a great blister until it finally burst into the sky in a spectacular double explosion of rocks, lava, ash, steam, and chunks of frozen earth. For weeks or even months, these great nostrils snorted fire and steam like the mother of all dragons. They blew volumes of fragmented basalt and pumice, as well as frozen lumps of gravel, sand, and sedimentary rock ripped from the throat of the volcano. And it expelled tephra, or volcanic ash. In the Devil Mountain Lakes eruption, the gritty, gray-brown tephra was composed mostly of volcanic glass, half of it silica.

As Hopkins poked and prodded the thawing and slumping banks of Devil Mountain Lakes in the summer of 1966, he noted in his field book "reddish plant debris—buried turf—willow leaf 1 cm long, grass sherds." And sitting on top of it, he noted, was "Devil Mtn ash." Hopkins stopped at intervals along the banks of the lake, collecting samples for pollen analysis, peat and twigs for radiocarbon dating. He returned to the area periodically over the years. In 1970, he spent most of the summer living in an old semiunderground, sod-roofed hut at the mouth of the Espenberg River. Also along were his daughter Chindi and a young colleague named Bob Rowland. Ned Goodhope, a local Eskimo, served as field assistant, and Gideon Barr, who had a reindeer camp on the Espenberg River, offered Hopkins the local knowledge of a natural-born natural historian. The group surveyed the small rivers between Goodhope Bay and Shishmaref Lagoon, sifting the sediments for seeds and beetle parts. They discovered that each of the five maar eruptions showed up in the layers of sediment as bands of tephra (volcanic ash). Hopkins had the elements of a great discovery, but he had not yet fit the clues together.

In 1974, a few years after Guthrie and Matthews published their Cape Deceit work, and as the productivity paradox battle raged, Hopkins again visited the maar lakes near Cape

In the summer of 1987, Hopkins worked on revising sea level history in Northwest Alaska with his protégé Julie Brigham-Grette. Here he inspects a buried ice layer on the beach near Teller *(Photo courtesy of Julie Brigham-Grette)*

Espenberg on northern Seward Peninsula. A floatplane dropped him off at an unnamed elongated little lake just southeast of Whitefish Lake, the most westerly of the Espenberg maars. After the pilot lifted off, Hopkins walked its shoreline. He scraped at the steep exposures where chunks of the high embankment had recently thawed and calved into the water. About four meters above the lake surface, he found a dark band of bedded tephra and beneath it, as he wrote in his field book, "buried turf, undulating surface with rooted twigs, in places continuous mat of 5-cm grass tufts." These he collected for radiocarbon dating.

Hopkins began to suspect that the tephra band from the maars' eruption was a broad, regional phenomenon (eventually he would discover that the ash blanketed hundreds of square miles of the northern Seward Peninsula). He realized that, once he dated the organic material below it, the ash layer could serve as a reference mark throughout the whole region. Wherever erosion exposed the earth to some depth—at a riverbank, a coastal cliff, or the edge of a lake—the ash band would run like a dateline between the layered strata.

The next day, Hopkins was again off by himself on the same little thaw lake. He noticed an exposure where a band of organic material could be seen. It included grass blades, moss, and some twigs, apparently rooted. "But no real peat or turf," as he wrote in his field book. "It seems more like detritus." Above this lay a foot and a half of ash, probably from the Whitefish Lake eruption. But as he started walking back to the other end of the lake, he stopped in his tracks. An idea struck him, which he promptly jotted down in his field notebook. "I don't think the 1-meter ash bed has anything to do with Whitefish Lake," he wrote. "Whitefish Lake is very old, but this ash is Wisconsin, and probably late Wisconsin. Maybe even Devil Mt. Ash."

The possibilities raced through his mind like the whirring icons of a slot machine. Then, one by one, they clicked into place. If the ash was from Devil Mountain, then the eruption was probably during Wisconsin time. Click. If Wisconsin time, then the land bridge was in place. Click. If the land bridge was in place, then the detritus covered by the ash was land bridge vegetation. Click. Jackpot!

It *wasn't* peat. It *was* detritus. It was an actual buried surface of the Bering Land Bridge, still there, intact, frozen in the permafrost beneath the gray tephra. Hopkins' mind bolted

Hopkins on a three-wheeler, Baldwin Peninsula, Northwest Alaska, 1987 *(Photo courtesy of Julie Brigham-Grette)*

ahead, sorting out how the ancient plant matter could have been preserved through the millennia. Where the ash layer accumulated to about three feet, the permafrost from the ground below rose up into the ash layer, freezing the former ground surface—puddles and all—beyond the reach of seasonal thaw. As he wrote it down, "the buried vegetation became frozen and remains beautifully preserved to the present day. In exposed sections, the seeds, leaves, and insects contained in the frozen peaty layers beneath each [maars'] ash fall provide a sampling of the local biota that lived just prior to the eruption—a valuable supplement to the less-detailed picture of the regional vegetation yielded by pollen in cores from the lake bottoms."

The ash proved to be from Devil Mountain, as Hopkins surmised, and when the laboratory returned dates for the plant

Hopkins discovered an actual surface of the land bridge, complete with plants frozen and buried under volcanic ash eighteen thousand years ago, at the height of the last glaciation *(Photo courtesy of Victoria Goetcheus Wolf)*

matter he had collected, the radiocarbon dates centered on about eighteen thousand years before present. As luck would have it, 18,000 years ago puts the eruption right about at the height of the last glacial period, the so-called "last glacial maximum." The eruption of the Devil Mountain maars occurred when the most recent land bridge was at its highest, driest, and widest. In short, the vegetation covered and preserved by the tephra, was *the* vegetation about which the palynologists and the vertebrate paleontologists had been arguing since the 1960s.

Hopkins knew that he needed a trained paleobotanist to assess the ancient plant remains. When he sat down to write up the results of his 1974 fieldwork, he made a point of recommending additional studies. No one came forward. After another visit to the area in 1988, he again sent out a call, hoping to lure a specialist to the buried surface, just as he had enticed Paul Colinvaux to drill a pollen core at Imuruk Lake. "A thorough study of the plant remains preserved beneath tephra beds in the Devil Mountain-Cape Espenberg area," he promised, "will be richly rewarding."

Hopkins was teaching at the University of Alaska Fairbanks in the 1990s when he interested a younger colleague named Mary Edwards in the problem, and together they took a few graduate students to the Devil Mountain Lakes region. With funding from the National Park Service, they undertook systematic sampling of the buried vegetation and soil. "Richly rewarded" they were. Whereas Paul Colinvaux used fossil pollen to infer the vegetation on the land bridge, and whereas Dale Guthrie proceeded from speculations about resident animals and their diets, now, with Hopkins' discovery, one could excavate, like an archeologist, the eighteen-thousand-year-old plant remains themselves. With shovel, trowel, and brush, Hopkins and colleagues did exactly that.

They found seeds, capsules, buds, stems, catkins, roots, moss, twigs, and leaves. They found extensive insect remains, a few rodent bones and dung, the nest of a singing vole, caribou pellets, and a bit of the skull cap and antler from a caribou. They found a flop of peaty material that might have passed through the digestive tract of a bison. They even found snow beds and frozen puddles with plants sticking straight through the ice. Hopkins thinks the explosions—there may have been many of them—probably occurred in the spring, May or June, because green-up had not yet taken place (as would be evident by July) and because the existence of puddles would indicate warm days. The vegetation looked like it had been steam rolled—like a fiber mat of crisscrossing stems and twigs, with willow leaves lying like projectile points and gray oval turds scattered about. It was as if a coverlet had been peeled back to reveal a day in the life of the Pleistocene. "It has this deep, rich smell," says Jeanne Schaaf, the Park Service sponsor of the project, "that's just a Pleistocene smell. I mean, you can almost sense the mammoth nearby."

Of course, the land beneath this tephra layer did not include every growing condition, and hence every vegetative mix, that might have existed over the entire continental expanse of Beringia. But the area covered was large; it was roughly at the center of the land bridge, north to south; it dated to the glacial maximum; and the plants were not being inferred, they were being *observed*. For evidence, it didn't get better than that. It was, in fact, unique in all the world.

Once harvested by the researchers, the ancient ground cover is none too prepossessing. Sitting in the refrigerators and freezers at a laboratory on the University of Alaska Fairbanks campus, plastic bags of the stuff look like pouches of soggy pipe tobacco. Lab technicians sieve and rinse and centrifuge the material according to their protocols until they have the plant macrofossils separated from the pollen, and both of these separated from soil and tephra. The pollen goes, with a drop or two of oil, into glass vials the size of a little finger. The pollen looks so fine it almost could be mistaken for a smudge. A lab worker puts a droplet of this mixture on a slide and uses a microscope to identify and count, one by one, each individual grain.

At another microscope, a technician uses a toothpick to pry apart what resembles the dregs of a teapot poured into a petri dish. Bit by bit, the material is segregated, seeds here, stems there, moss over there. White plastic saucers hold submerged seeds and seed sacks, sorted by taxa. Under a bright light and magnification, they take on strange shapes. The seed and sack of *Potentilla* looks like an umber-colored brain, dimly visible through a tanniferous skull. *Draba's* yellow-brown seed sack has a hinged door that stands open, like the head of a spawned-out salmon, hooked jaw agape. And the seeds of *Kobresia*, an alpine sedge, sport tails like a race of brown tadpoles.

Hopkins' two graduate students, Claudia Höfle and Victoria Goetcheus*, agreed the eruption occurred in spring. That would account for the buried ice they found in low spots and the intact nest of a singing vole. The subnivian (under-snow) nest might retain its shape for a little while after emerging from the melting snow in the spring, but the bits of plant litter and dung likely would have been scattered if the summer had been more advanced when the ash fell. As to whether the plant litter might have been concentrated due to transportation by wind, Goetcheus, writing in 1995, concluded the leaf fragments found on the buried surface were not the sort likely to have been blown far by wind, but rather were likely to have fallen where they grew. Writing in the same year, Claudia Höfle, a soil scientist, finds that the extensive network of fine roots—incontestably in situ remains—are indicative of abundant herbaceous vegetation.

Goetcheus reconstructs the plant community as including a continuous understory of various mosses above which grasses and sedges, notably *Kobresia*, flourished. Diverse herbaceous plants covered twenty-five to forty percent of each sample area. Willows showed up at only three sites, but covered thirty to fifty percent of those areas, apparently taking advantage of depressions where runoff might collect or shaded areas where

*Now Victoria Goetcheus Wolf.

snowbanks would persist. Plant cover frequently exceeded a hundred percent due to the layering of plants of different heights. The mix of taxa suggests a dry tundra, with intermittent willow, but abundant grasses and forbs, most of which are known to favor or require a calcium-rich soil. Höfle thinks that the frequent deposition of windblown silt may have accounted for the presence of this mineral nutrient.

The dominance of herbaceous plants in a dry place might be explained, Hopkins and his colleagues reason, by a seasonal climate pattern whereby the soil absorbed precipitation in the fall, froze, then thawed out wet in the spring, giving plants a good start. An abundance of roots suggests a moist but well aerated soil. The constant sifting down of wind-transported silt may have been a key variable in supporting soil fertility and a relatively rich herbaceous plant community.

Taken together, these results indicate that the central uplands of the last land bridge, in what today is northern Seward Peninsula, was a dry meadow and herb-rich tundra where a mix of grasses and herbs, notably the sedge *Kobresia*, along with occasional willow, flourished atop a continuous understory of mosses. And, while no precise modern analog exists, the vegetation, root network, and soil characteristics best fit a cold, dry, Arctic steppe community. That this mix of *Kobresia*-dominated vegetation could have fed the grazing ungulates of the Pleistocene has been shown by direct evidence: the stomach contents of frozen mummies.

Additional studies, no doubt, will modify and refine this picture. But Hopkins believes that ecological conditions on the last Bering Land Bridge seem to have been sufficient to support herds of grazing animals, as well as the predators who preyed on them. And those conditions, in turn, would have permitted the land bridge to be inhabited by humans.

# 13

# THE FIRST AMERICANS

On Tuesday morning, November 3, 1964, Louis Giddings drove his Volkswagen bus north along the peninsula that separates Narragansett Bay from Mount Hope Bay in eastern Rhode Island. He was heading in to Providence from his house at Bristol, on the grounds of Brown University's Haffenreffer Museum. Giddings was both the director of the Haffenreffer and Brown's first professor of anthropology. He motored along a couple of miles of winding country road, then down four miles of highway before he entered Interstate Route 195, which bee-lines into Providence from the southeast. At three-fifths of a mile west of the Seenkonk-Rehoboth town line, Giddings' VW bus came abreast of another vehicle traveling in the same direction. Ahead of both of them was an Army truck towing a jeep. A newspaper account does not state which driver lost control. What is known is that a sideswipe collision occurred that sent both cars careening against the Army vehicles. In what the state police would call a "spectacular" crash, the truck and attached jeep veered into an embankment, while Giddings' bus flipped and skidded on its side for some one hundred twenty feet.

Kate Carlisle, Giddings' niece attended Brown at the time. She said the bus had seat belts, but her uncle wasn't wearing his. "We went to the junkyard after the accident to get some

Louis Giddings, probably in the early 1960s, probably in Northwest Alaska (*Photo courtesy of Laboratory of Tree Ring Research, University of Arizona)*

stuff out of the van, and the passenger's side was totaled, but the driver's side did not look too bad." Tossed around inside the van, Giddings smashed his head, collarbone, elbow, and hands, at least. Carlisle remembers "many broken bones, ribs, punctured lung." Nevertheless, Giddings fought his way back from the serious injuries. After five weeks in the hospital, his greatest worry was that his recuperation might jeopardize the coming summer's field schedule. He was looking forward to "a joyous return to the Kobuk" and his diggings at Onion Portage, as he wrote in his memoir. "He looked like hell," said Kate, "but he was so ready to come home. I remember the joy and anticipation of him finally being able to come home." A couple of days before he was to be discharged to home care, Giddings got out of bed to walk the halls a bit. Apparently, the activity shook loose a blood clot. When it reached his heart, it killed him instantly, says his niece. "I remember being in total shock. I kept saying, 'But he was coming home, how could he be dead?' It was very sad."

Sad for the family, for the whole Arctic community, and for Hopkins in particular. Hopkins and Giddings had been at work on their second collaborative paper (this time joined by the geologist Troy Péwé), again blending the disciplines of geology

Hopkins at Nunyano, Chukotka, looking back across Bering Strait to Alaska, 1992 *(Photo courtesy of Julie Brigham-Grette)*

and archeology. Giddings' secretary and editorial assistant, Marjorie Tomas, wrote Hopkins on December 9, 1964, to say that she had just that morning been working on refinements to the abstract. "Before I finished, Mrs. Giddings called with the crushing news that Dr. Giddings died a few hours ago—a massive heart attack which could only be attributable to his injuries. My grief is too great to attempt any more with the abstract. Please do whatever you can with it. ..."

Hopkins rewrote the piece and offered Giddings' wife, Bets, any help he could give. Because she was an anthropologist and her husband's close professional associate, and to ensure the continuation of Giddings' work and ideas, the university appointed Bets to her husband's position as director of the Haffenreffer Museum. Brown also named Giddings' former professor at both the University of Alaska and the University of Pennsylvania, Froelich Rainey, as overall director of the Onion Portage excavations. To direct the day-to-day dig, the university selected Giddings' graduate student and field assistant, Douglas Anderson, with Bets Giddings to work as his field assistant.

Mrs. Giddings wrote Hopkins: "There are few to whom [Louis] talked so much about the scope of his work. You were the one geologist whose work and word he appreciated most." She wondered if Hopkins could manage a visit to Onion Portage during the coming summer to help puzzle out the geology. Hopkins flew out to the Kobuk River, looked over the site, and wrote an outline of the geology for the Brown group. When they sought renewed funding to continue the dig, Hopkins helped there too, writing the National Science Foundation that he thought Onion Portage was one of the "most interesting and important archeological sites in Alaska" and that its excavation "must be pressed vigorously."

By the time Doug Anderson had reached the bottommost

cultural layer at Onion Portage, the excavation begun by Giddings had uncovered more than thirty cultural layers descending in distinct stratigraphy for an incredible eighteen vertical feet. Henry Collins, the Smithsonian Institution's eminent Eskimo archeologist, called Onion Portage "undoubtedly the most important archeological site ever found in the Arctic."

With his friend Louis Giddings gone, Hopkins took his questions about human migration to William Laughlin, whom he had known at Harvard. A physical anthropologist by training, Laughlin had worked among the Aleut people since he was of high school age, traveling to the Aleutian Islands with the famous physician-turned-anthropologist, Ales Hrdlicka. In the 1960s, at the time of his contribution to Hopkins' first land bridge book, Laughlin was working on Umnak Island, at the eastern end of the Aleutian chain. During the glacial period, Umnak was the western terminus of an expanded and lengthened Alaska peninsula. More than that, because the water off the western tip of Umnak is deep just offshore, this portion of the island has nearly the same coastline now as it did when the last land bridge existed. Because it commanded the entrance to the Bering Sea, Laughlin says, Umnak was an ecological magnet, attracting both sea mammals and humans.

Laughlin thought that the mongoloid Asians—ancestors of the Aleuts and Eskimos—entered the land bridge as permanent residents, not as migrants making a crossing. Migration was the eventual effect, but so too was the establishment of permanent occupation, which Laughlin believes has persisted continuously to the present day. Coastal dwellers, without moving very far, could hunt on the land, the sea, and the rivers. After sea levels stabilized, they also had the great advantage of a rich and easily exploited intertidal zone. When the tide was out, sea urchins, limpets, whelks, mussels, chitons, clams, kelp, seaweed, and edible algae could be gathered in baskets, while octopus and some fish could be taken with a gaff hook or spear from the crevices in the exposed reefs. A simple technology of dip nets, set nets, fish spears, and hooks could account for abundant food. Moreover, the harvesting could be done by the least hardy members of the group: women, children, and old people. Most important of all, these sources of food were available nearly year-round, as recurrent as the tide.

Such a buffer against starvation may have afforded coastal residents of the land bridge the leisure to develop the use of boats, leading to what Laughlin calls "an engineering triumph": the kayak. The coracle (a small, open, and rounded skin boat) or the umiak (a larger skin boat able to hold many men) permitted hunters to range out to the fringes of offshore islands. Here were additional intertidal zones and reefs, as well as fox-proof nesting cliffs for seabirds. The kittiwakes, eiders, cormorants, puffins, ducks, and gulls could provide hundreds of dozens of eggs, and feathery skins for lightweight and warm parkas. But the more seaworthy kayak, with its covered deck, permitted hunters to travel further, to chase and lance marine mammals, including the humpback whales, fur seals, sea lions, porpoises, and sea otters. "A natural progression of greater rewards for improved technology exists in the coastal area," wrote Laughlin. "Each additional step, from strand hunting and collecting, through use of a simple coracle, through use of a boat with keelson (umiak), and finally to the kayak—and with it the culmination of open sea hunting—adds another series of exploitational areas."

Laughlin was, above all, a human ecologist, says Hopkins. "His thinking has always been concerned with what the people were doing, what their resources were." Hopkins says he learned by listening to what Laughlin knew, but also from what he did not know, by looking into the kinds of questions Laughlin asked him. Were there, for example, low, flat areas along the coast during land bridge times, marshy areas where migratory birds might fatten up? "He wanted to know what the productivity would have been along the shore of the land bridge because it's his postulate that the Anangula [Umnak area] people were the most ancient known people of the Aleutians and that they dispersed along the shore of the land bridge."

In Hopkins' 1967 book, Laughlin observed the differences between the coastal Aleuts and Eskimos on the one hand, and the interior Indians on the other. Research into the morphology, serology, archeology, and linguistics of the two groups suggested to Laughlin that there had been two waves of migration across Beringia, one coastal and the other inland. But in the years since Hopkins has been closely involved in human migration researches, there have been some interesting convergences of thought. Notably, some workers in the fields of linguistics, genetics, and dentition (the study of teeth) suggest that there were not two, but three migrations over the land bridge. And that explanation fits pretty well with archeological and geological evidence.

Teeth turn out to be good indicators of a population's history. Cultural traits, like a particular technique for knocking out stone tools, can be passed to unrelated groups and may not be indicative of a common genetic heritage at all. Even when these practices have not been exchanged between groups, there still can be remarkable resemblances in the fabrication of houses or of hats or of fishhooks simply because of the common objective, the similarity of materials at hand, and similar problem solving strategies. Genetic traits are much better indicators of relatedness, but even they are problematic. If a given trait depends on the inheritance of a single gene, and if it has a low frequency of occurrence in a population, then a small migrating band may not happen to include any individuals with that particular gene. Native Americans, for example, lack the B blood type, even though it is present in their presumed ancestral stock in Northeast Asia. The explanation may be that, just by chance, the colonizing band of migrants happened not to have among them anyone with the less frequently occurring B blood type, accounting for the trait not showing up today among their New World descendants. So the best clues are genetic traits that depend on many genes and do not change readily in response to use, diet, health, or other environmental factors. "Teeth," says Christy Turner, who has studied the teeth of more than nine thousand skulls, "meet these requirements." Teeth preserve extraordinarily well, outlasting bones. And teeth can be dated.

Back in the 1920s, when Laughlin's teacher Ales Hrdlicka was analyzing the morphological traits of Native American bones, he noticed they frequently showed a "shovel" shape on the tongue side of the upper incisors. Ridges on the outside margins of those teeth give them the scoop shape of a square shovel. Turner found additional tooth characteristics that differ between groups but that do not change much over time. They include the number of roots, the number of cusps on the molars, a feature called Carabelli's cusp on the first upper molar, and what he calls "winging" of the central incisors (where they are cocked at an angle to one another, rather than arrayed in a straight line, shoulder to shoulder). Different groups possess each of these traits to varying degrees. No single trait is diagnostic, but a groups' dental signature can be defined statistically.

Turner finds two dental patterns among Mongoloid Asian peoples. The older one shows up in Southeast Asia between about seventeen thousand and thirty thousand years ago around the Sunda Shelf, a now submerged continental plain that formerly bridged the islands and the mainland of Southeast Asia. The Sundadont pattern, as Turner has named it, expanded along the coast into the islands of Japan. It also spread north and inland into what is today China and Mongolia. And this branch evolved a new dental pattern that Turner calls Sinodont. Sinodonts show more shoveling, winging, and three-rooted lower first molars than do the Sundadonts. The changes could have evolved in response to the colder, more stressful conditions of the north, says Turner, but more likely they were simply random genetic changes. In any event, he concludes that the dental evidence is clear: "the ancestors of all living Native Americans came from Northeast Asia." Identifying this area as the ancestral locale of Native Americans was not original, but Turner's arrival at that interpretation via dental evidence was.

Meanwhile, Stanford University's Joseph Greenberg reached a similar conclusion following a completely independent line of inquiry. He relied not on what was in the mouth, but on what came out of it. A linguist, Greenberg had done monumental and widely acclaimed work sorting out the languages of Africa. Then he turned his attention to Native American languages, which probably numbered more than a thousand when Columbus landed. It seemed logical to investigators that the variety of languages had evolved from a single one spoken by the first pioneering inhabitants of the New World. Proponents of man's great antiquity in the Americas considered that it would take as long as a hundred thousand years of residency for the root language to splinter into this bewildering array of distinct variations.

But Greenberg was less interested in trying to predict a rate of divergence than in classifying the languages according to their kinship. One early anthropologist, John Wesley Powell, the famous explorer of the Grand Canyon, had segregated fifty-eight families of Native American languages. Later investigators, finding more similarities, pared that number down, but not to the extent that Greenberg did. According to Greenberg, there were only three core languages. He applied a list of three hundred cognates (words held in common) to Native American languages. They were words unlikely to change much, like the words for body parts or grammatical parts, like first and second person pronouns. He found that there were enough interrelationships among the hundreds of Native American languages that they could be grouped into three families: Eskimo-Aleut, Na-Dene, and Amerind. The Eskimo-Aleut family contained ten languages, including Inuit-Inupiaq, spoken across the Arctic coasts from Alaska to Greenland; Yupik, spoken along the Bering Sea and North Pacific coasts; and Aleut, the language of the Aleutian Islands people. In the Na-Dene family group, Greenberg identified thirty-eight languages, including those of the Athabascan people of interior Alaska and northwest Canada, with outliers in California, as well as the related Navaho and Apache speakers of the American Southwest. The Amerind family includes all the other Native American languages spoken from Canada to the tip of Chile, over nine hundred in all.

Greenberg believes that the differences between the three linguistic groups is so pronounced, so to speak, that they must trace back to distinct Old World populations, and that each of these must have crossed the land bridge at a different time. The first migration should have been the Amerind linguistic group, because it occupies the southernmost geography (South America), and its languages are the least similar to those found in the Old World, having had more time to differentiate into local variants. Next to arrive must have been the Na-Dene family, which has a more southerly center of gravity than the Eskimo-Aleut family and which retains some connection with Asian languages, while having undergone more internal differentiation than Eskimo-Aleut. Last to cross into the New World, the Eskimo-Aleut family shows close affinities with Siberian and Old World languages and occupies the regions nearest the land bridge.

Of course, like toolmaking techniques, words can be borrowed by one culture from another, whether or not the two groups share common ancestry. However, for the most part, Greenberg's linguistics-derived reconstruction of the migration fits nicely with Turner's dentition-derived theory: three groups and three migrations. They differ as to who came second. Turner believes the Aleut-Eskimos arrived before the Na-Dene people.

Hoping to bring a third discipline to bear on the question, Greenberg and Turner teamed up with a geneticist named Stephen Zegura. Unlike language or toolmaking habits, the similarity of certain genetic traits necessarily indicates a shared ancestry, rather than a response to environmental conditions. Zegura looked at blood group antigens, serum proteins, erythrocyte enzymes, immunoglobulins, leukocyte antigens, and mitochondrial DNA, among other genetic material. The picture is not clear, he says, as to where the Amerind populations fit in genetically. The Na-Dene are problematic too, showing some affinities with the Amerind and some with the Eskimo-Aleut.

Zegura thinks his genetic data are supportive of the three-migration theory, though not confirmatory. He points to the long-term work of Robert Williams and coworkers as the best support from genetics. Williams' team analyzed genetic markers from thousands of Native Americans. Those typed fell into two pre-European–contact groups. The first was comprised of Apache and Navajo (both Athabascan speakers). The second group included members of the Amerind, to use Greenberg's term. That left the Eskimo, but they were not part of this study. The groupings produced by genetic typing led Williams' team to concur that there were three migrations across the land bridge: paleo-Indians (Amerinds) first; Athabascan speakers (including the Navajo and Apache) second; and last, the Eskimo and Aleuts.

Another corroborating bit of evidence comes from considering how long it might have taken for today's divergent dental patterns, language variations, or genetic traits to develop. It's rather hypothetical, but the three specialists come up with similar timetables for the postulated three pulses of migration: around thirteen thousand years ago, around ten thousand years ago, and around four thousand years ago. And, they claim, this chronology matches up nicely with geological and archeological data. Geologically, they say the land bridge was in place before about ten thousand years ago (other researchers estimate the date of submergence to be eleven thousand to fourteen thousand years ago) for a period of perhaps fifteen thousand years (others think much longer), permitting migration without the use of boats, for which there is little evidence. Archeologically, Turner, Greenberg, and Zegura believe, the record is also supportive. Before people could migrate across the land bridge, they had to be established in Eastern Siberia, and until recently there was no record of human occupation east of Lake Baikal before twenty thousand years ago. Even a newly reported find of thirty-thousand-year-old tools in the Yana River Valley, while pushing back the earliest known date of human occupation of the Asian Arctic some sixteen thousand years, still places humans fifteen hundred miles from Bering Strait. Probably around fourteen thousand years ago, toolmakers linked to the Na-Dene were present at Diuktai along the Aldan River of Eastern Siberia, and they show up in Kamchatka at about the same time. They produced a range of implements, including bifacial knives and points, microblades likely inset into shafts, as well as bone and ivory artifacts.

Of course, not everyone agrees—about anything. Greenberg predicted that colleagues would greet his classification system with "something akin to outrage." They did. Most experts denounced his methodology and conclusions. Even the least obstreperous of his critics consider Greenberg's classification well out in front of the available evidence, as the discussion continues. Turner's dental evidence likewise has holes in it or, as David Meltzer calls them, "cavities." Turner's groups are not discrete and internally consistent. Aleut teeth do not group as well with Eskimo teeth, where Turner places them, as they do with Na-Dene teeth, where he says they do not belong. Some Na-Dene teeth from coastal areas are less similar to Na-Dene from the interior than they are to Eskimo-Aleut teeth. As Meltzer writes, "So goes the dental evidence, neither a direct record of migration nor tightly linked to identifiable groups, nor (so far at least) producing internally homogeneous groups." Ongoing work by Douglas Wallace and colleagues involving mitochondrial DNA indicates that Na-Dene are genetically distinct from Amerinds and that the Amerinds show a longer history of separation from Old World ancestral stock. Where the Eskimo-Aleuts fit is still unresolved. Wallace's work does support Turner and Greenberg's theory that Amerinds derive from a single pulse of Asian immigrants.

Regardless of all that might be learned from these studies, it is entirely possible that the very first Americans did not successfully establish themselves for the long term, that they died off without leaving a lineage, that they are ancestors to no one. In that case, neither their language, nor their teeth, nor their genes will show up in contemporary Native Americans. Only one science has a chance of uncovering relics of their residence in the New World: archeology.

# 14

# THE FIRST OF THE FIRST

The University of Alaska Fairbanks, with its broad range of graduate programs, is the state's principal academic institution and a center for Beringian scholarship. Scores of professors and researchers study land bridge geology, paleontology, palynology, archeology, anthropology, and other areas. Nevertheless, one of the most significant land bridge discoveries credited to the university emerged not from its laboratories or libraries, but from the ground on which the buildings stood.

On a fall day in 1933, a student named James Jacobsen was digging a posthole for the freshman bonfire at the Alaska Agricultural College and School of Mines as it was called then. The school sits on a bluff, and Jacobsen was digging at the crest of it, a scant hundred yards from the administration building. It was always a good spot from which to look out over the Chena and Tanana River valleys. Proof of that turned up in Jacobsen's shovel in the form of a flint projectile point.

The following summer, two students decided to dig a forty-foot test cut at the site and located "a surprising concentration of worked stone material." They packed about four hundred of the artifacts into a gallon can and sent it to Nels Nelson, an archeologist at the American Museum of Natural History. Nelson had been on an expedition to Mongolia and recognized the small flint cores and flakes as "identical in several respects with thousands of specimens found in the Gobi desert." Dating the Campus site artifacts to seven thousand to ten thousand years old, Nelson declared, "The specimens furnish the first clear archaeological evidence we have of early migration to the American continent." A later investigator, Charles Mobley, recognized the artifacts as similar to those unearthed in Siberia, northern China, and Japan. The Campus site was, he said, "the first evidence in support of the Bering Land Bridge hypothesis for human entrance into North America from Asia."

Today, most archeologists, including Mobley, consider the site to be only three thousand to four thousand years old. In any event, it furnished Alaska's first recognized microblades and Alaska's largest collection of cores. Although some of the artifacts are no doubt still intact at the site, today people drive cars over it. In 1966, the university president, William R. Wood, announced the selection of the Campus site as the location for a new visitor's lookout—complete with a large totem pole—to be adjacent to a new road, sidewalks, and a parking lot. Though archeologists from several states and countries strongly objected, Wood insisted on the development. Eventually, the university removed the totem pole, a relic of maritime societies and a cultural square peg in interior Alaska. The asphalt, however, remains.

The Campus site stood virtually alone as an archeological link between Alaska and Siberia until Hopkins explored the Trail Creek Caves, leading to Helge Larsen's excavation there in 1949 and 1950. Larsen found more of the tiny flakes of stone the archeologists were calling microblades, as well as the cores from which they were struck. In the lowest levels of one cave, he also found bone projectile points. Slots in the points corresponded exactly to the dimensions of the microblades, which apparently were intended as insets to provide razor-sharp cutting edges along the sides of the point. This was the first, and remains one of the only, discoveries in eastern Beringia of slotted bone points together with microblades. The fashioning of microblades was an ingenious way to utilize what was perhaps the world's first precious stone, says archeologist E. James Dixon. A pound of stone rendered into microblades, he says, could yield over five hundred linear inches of cutting edge, versus about eight linear inches of edge if a conventional point were fabricated from the same pound. And this efficiency was especially important in the far North, where snow covered the ground for about eight months of the year, making it difficult to locate suitable rock.

Additional microblades and cores turned up in the 1960s when Frederick West excavated a number of sites in and around the Alaska Range. He grouped these with Trail Creek into a single tradition he called the Denali complex, after the Athabascan name for Mt. McKinley, the highest peak in North America. Searching for prototype traditions in Siberia, West found that Russian workers at the Dyuktai site in the Lake Baikal region had unearthed similar tools. Denali's relationship to Dyuktai is clearly, writes West, "that of direct derivative."

In the Nenana River Valley in interior Alaska, a cluster of deeply stratified sites has produced Clovi.slike tools dated to eleven thousand three hundred years before present. And similar implements have been found in Siberia's Kamchatka Peninsula. The earliest well dated evidence of human occupation in Alaska came from a handful of sites in the Tanana River valley, upriver from Fairbanks. The oldest of them is the Broken Mammoth site, situated on a bluff overlooking both the Tanana River and Shaw Creek Flats, where microblades, scrapers, stone and ivory points, eyed needles, and other artifacts date to eleven thousand eight hundred years ago. Along with the tools, archeologists found the bones of bison, elk, caribou, and sheep, as well as those of swans, geese, ducks, ptarmigan, and other birds, ground squirrel, red squirrel, porcupine, marmot, snowshoe hare, and fish. This wealth of small animal remains suggests a rich late glacial environment and proves that these late Pleistocene hunters practiced a diversified economy and made their living from more than big game alone. Similar arrays of eleven-thousand-year-old animal bones show up on Siberia's Kamchatka Peninsula. And toolmaking patterns there replicate some of those found in the Nenana Valley.

Among archeologists, it's the rare scholar who is without a trowel to grind, and one who can sift through the information and provide a synthesis in plain English. One of them is David Meltzer, a writer, professor, and field archeologist who studied the paleoecology of Beringia under Hopkins. Twenty thousand years ago, Meltzer believes, Native Americans were part of a single ancestral stock in northeast Asia, as their teeth and genetic markers reveal. All possessed the Sinodont dental morphology. But they had begun to diverge genetically into distinct groups before moving east onto the land bridge, and they continued to differentiate in the New World. Linguistic and dental evidence conflicts as to whether the Na-Dene or the Eskimo-Aleut were the second to arrive, but they strongly suggest that the first Asians to enter the Western Hemisphere were the Amerinds. Their ancestors chipped stone tools in Eastern Siberia later than twenty thousand years ago, perhaps as recently as fourteen thousand years ago. And similar tools appear in Alaska at least by eleven thousand five hundred years ago, as the land bridge submerged at the end of the Ice Age. Amerinds may have aggregated in unglaciated central Alaska for a few millennia, until a way through the glaciers to the south opened up. With the Laurentide and Cordilleran Ice Sheets shrinking toward their centers, an ice-free corridor must have opened up between them. While it may not have looked like a frozen version of the Red Sea parting for the fleeing Israelites, some kind of passageway would have appeared, and it may have accommodated Amerind people expanding southward into latitudes that are more temperate.

Or all that could be wrong. As Meltzer points out, some of the oldest dated sites in the New World turn up in *South* America.

Chilean workmen clearing brush in 1976 for a road across Chinchihuapi Creek unearthed bones that, once examined at the Universidad Austral de Chile, proved to be from mastodon. Tom Dillehay, an American archeologist then teaching there, concluded that the bones showed signs of butchering by humans. When Dillehay visited the site, called Monte Verde, he found wooden implements and even mastodon meat and skin preserved in the boggy soil. As the dig continued along thirteen hundred feet of stream bank, workers unearthed twelve dwellings, three human footprints, hearths lined with clay and thirty-eight hunks of meat. They discovered a great variety of plants, including four kinds of seaweed, carried to the site from the Pacific coast, thirty river miles away, and plants from distant grasslands, even the Andean highlands. There were eleven varieties of wild potato, twenty-three kinds of medicinal plants, seeds, fruit, and leaves that had been chewed. Of tools, they found lances, digging sticks, and a few stone implements. One bifacial point was made of quartzite from a range of mountains thirty-seven miles away. But, most amazing of all, Dillehay radiocarbon dated the occupation surface to about twelve thousand five hundred years ago, a thousand years older than the oldest Clovis site in North America.

If the theory is correct that Beringian hunters migrated south through a deglaciated corridor eleven thousand five hundred years ago to people the Americas, how is it that Monte Verde—ten thousand miles farther south—was inhabited a thousand years earlier? A number of scholars think they have an answer. One of them is E. James Dixon, who was a young graduate student when Hopkins invited him along to the Khabarovsk conference in Siberia and who remembered the Russians chanting, "Hop-kins, Hop-kins." Dixon has been digging in caves on Prince of Wales Island in the Tongass Forest of Southeast Alaska. In one, he found human bones that, when radiocarbon dated, turned out to be the oldest reliably dated early man bones ever found in Alaska or Canada: ninety-two hundred years before present. The cave, whose name is being kept secret in deference to the wishes of the local Native people, also contained a ten-thousand-three-hundred-year-old bone implement, as well as stone tools. The limestone basement of the many islands of the Tongass Forest contains hundreds of caves. Dixon anticipates more discoveries: "It's my belief that some of the oldest archaeological remains preserved in North America may be found in the caves of Southeast Alaska." The coastal areas are rich, he says, "The table's set twice a day—at low tide, and again at low tide." All of this suggests to Dixon that the first Americans followed a route through Beringia, all right, but along the coast, in boats.

Textbooks usually depict the entire northwest coast of North America as completely covered by ice during the Ice Age. The ice sheet drops from the adjacent mountains of Alaska and Canada right into the sea, perhaps out to the edge of the continental shelf. But Dixon believes there were strips of unglaciated land along the coastal plain. These areas would have been warmer because of the low elevation and the heat-retaining properties of the sea. During the late Ice Age, possibly as early as fourteen thousand years ago, these refugia would have permitted a seagoing people equipped with boats to fish, hunt sea mammals, and forage the tidal flats. These people, Dixon believes, were the first to colonize the New World, spreading south along the west coast of both Americas. And with the vast Pacific on their right, glaciers on their left, and already populated areas to the north, there may have been good reason to hasten south.

Dixon wasn't the first to come up with this idea. That distinction belongs to the Canadian researcher, Knut Fladmark, who established the geological possibility of a coastal route into the Americas, though he never claimed to have proven that it happened. In fact, many archeologists consider the "maritime entry" model problematic. For one thing, solid evidence of late Pleistocene sea mammal hunting (as distinct from seaworthy boats) is minimal. For another, northeast Asian maritime cultures developed significantly *later* than northwest North American maritime cultures. Alaskan archeologist William Workman, who has dug for years along the coast, is one of the skeptics. "If Pleistocene maritime colonists came from northeast Asia, their skills were forgotten, to be painfully reinvented in the middle Holocene," he says. "Possible, I suppose, but it seems unlikely to me." Of the coastal route theory, Workman says, "Fladmark demonstrated this was possible, but in recent years a possibility has been promoted first to a probability, then to a near certainty, without excessive input of convincing data."

Humans did somehow cross open ocean to reach Australia more than forty thousand years ago. But that was probably done in rafts. And transoceanic raft travel in the South Pacific is an altogether different proposition from crossing the glacier-fringed waters of the Gulf of Alaska in the North Pacific. Still, if the people reaching coastal Siberia twenty thousand years ago had developed watercraft such as skin boats, their expansion around the Pacific Rim—from Kamchatka to South America—could have taken place with lightning speed and before appreciable expansion inland. And that could account, proponents believe, for older artifacts turning up in the southern reaches of the New World, even before the barrier glaciers had melted.

But for every theory, there is a countertheory, and the intensity of the debate is marked. Sorting out all the archeological, geological, paleontological, palynological, paleoenvironmental, linguistic, genetic, and dental clues of the great migration, says E. James Dixon, permits us to understand deep issues having to do with "the nature of humans as colonizers, their impact on pristine environments, and the influence of different environments on cultural development." And, as Dixon's former mentor Hopkins would add, it's also a lot of fun. The coastwise migration theory that Dixon endorses does not contradict the classical idea of Siberians walking dry-shod across the land bridge from Asia into North America, he says. Rather, he sees coastal Beringia as the fastest route into the New World, the one taken by the first of the first Americans. Beringia is still the northern filter through which all New World migrants passed. And Hopkins, he says, is still "the leading international expert on the history of the Bering Land Bridge," the one scholar who held all the strands of Beringia studies in his hand, who, metaphorically, raised Beringia up out of the depths until we could almost see it.

# 15

# THE LAST OF THE LAST

There is nothing picturesque about a five A.M. midwinter drive along Airport Way in Fairbanks, Alaska. Darkness crowds the eerie light of sodium-burning street lamps into ghostly yellow spheres, and a roaring heater fan does battle with the forty-below air on the other side of the glass. But the ice fog won't set in until later when the traffic increases, and the signal lights at this hour are set to favor the arterial. It's a clear shot across town to the clinic, where a few lights show in the southeast corner of the fourth floor. The dialysis ward.

In the room are a dozen people who have risen early to come here for a four-hour session. They lie back in recliners. Some read, some doze. The lights are kept low, except beside the readers. The room seems unnaturally quiet. It looks like a middle-of-the-night scene on board one of the Alaska state ferryboats, where passengers sleep in lounge chairs. From the radial artery in the forearm of each person, blood passes via tubing to a hemodialysis machine the size of a small refrigerator. The machine filters the wastes and pumps the blood back into a vein. Hopkins is one of the readers: *Things Seen and Unseen*, a metaphysical work by Nora Gallagher, his stepson's wife.

Hopkins retired from the U.S. Geological Survey in Menlo Park, California, in 1984 after forty-two years' service, to accept a position at the University of Alaska Fairbanks as Distinguished Professor of Quaternary Studies and Director of the Alaska Quaternary Center. By the late 1980s, a variety of health problems limited his ability to continue with the rigors of fieldwork. But those who have worked with him over the years carry in their minds images of Hopkins following his interests into rugged country despite increasing limitations as he aged.

Jeanne Schaaf of the National Park Service worked with Hopkins in the late stages of his career on Seward Peninsula. She remembers a trip with him on a river that the white Park Service folks call the Nugnugaluktuk (and with pretty good pronunciation) but that the Eskimos call simply the Lane River, after a resident family. On this particular trip in the 1980s, Hopkins insisted on doing various taxing chores, including helping to lug the boat up onto the beach. "And that resulted in him repeatedly popping his urostomy bags," says Schaaf, "until he was down to his last one." Urostomy bags are a scarce commodity on the Nugnugaluktuk, so Schaaf hopped in a Park Service plane and flew to Nome to see about finding some. There were none, not even at the hospital. By the time she called her husband in Anchorage, it was late in the evening. Driving around Anchorage that night, Robert Schaaf tried several closed pharmacies before finding one that, though locked, had someone inside. Negotiations ensued through the glass door. The pharmacist, it seemed, had a lot of raffle tickets to sell. Waving greenbacks, Robert Schaaf declared a keen interest in the fundraiser, one of his favorite charities. The glass door opened. The next jet to Nome carried the bags, and Hopkins was spared having to come up with a field remedy that likely would have involved duct tape and garbage bags. He so enjoyed this trip that the following year he made up his mind to take his doctor's advice and undergo a heart valve replacement operation that would allow him to do more fieldwork.

In the summer of 1992 Julie Brigham-Grette and Patricia Heiser, then doctoral students studying under Hopkins, accompanied him on a field trip to the Chukotka Peninsula on the Russian side of Bering Strait. Besides the three Americans, the party included several Russians. On July 15, just as the wind picked up and the weather took a turn for the worse, the Russians decided to move camp about fifteen miles up the coast. They tied two inflatable lifeboats together with scrap lumber into a makeshift catamaran. It wasn't the most seaworthy craft, with the two boats shifting differentially in the rough seas. With only a fifteen-horse outboard for power, the trip took several tense hours. The waves grew, and the wind flung spray, icy reminders of the frigid Bering Sea beneath.

When they arrived at the new spot, the tide had fallen, and rocks prevented an easy landing at the campsite. Jumping out, and slipping on the kelp and rocks, all hands lined the boats in to where they could be unloaded. It bruised his pride, says Hopkins, when one of the women saw him tugging feebly on the bowline and said, "Let me take that, Dave." Ashore, Hopkins started up the steep bank with a pack and a duffle, but he was having trouble. He dropped the duffle, and one of the Russians took his pack. He looked ashen, exhausted, and stressed. The others helped him set up his tent and installed him in it. For two days he lay there, too weak to do anything more, while the wind and rain lashed "like a hurricane," he says. His colleagues began to think that something more serious than exhaustion was the matter. They wondered about a heart attack, knowing that he'd undergone angioplasty procedures six times, and finally had a stent put in. It seemed best to get him to a doctor. But the rough weather had worsened. Besides the cold and wind, the waves that pounded offshore now were too big for the boats. That night, two of the Russian scientists, Victor Ivanov and Boris Buktopochi set out on foot for the tiny village of Enmelen, six or seven miles away.

Enmelen was so small, it did not even have an airstrip. There was a satellite phone, and the scientists requested a helicopter from Providenya. A woman named Sakalova, who said she was a doctor, accompanied the men back to camp in a huge Russian truck with fat tundra tires. They arrived at three o'clock in the morning. Sakalova asked Hopkins to open his shirt so she could massage his heart. As Hopkins and his students exchanged nervous glances, the woman held her hands a few inches above his chest and manipulated them just as if she were kneading bread. She never actually touched him, and the operation struck the American scientists as altogether eerie, as if they'd been transported to the place and time they'd been searching for: They were huddled, stormbound on the land bridge, the everlasting Arctic wind rattling a frail tent, while a mysterious shaman conjured an ancient magic.

The wind raged through the night. In the morning, no helicopter appeared. Brigham-Grette had been on lots of field trips with Hopkins to remote places in Alaska, dropped off for days without a radio. She began to recall times when the two of them had discussed the risk of Hopkins having a heart attack when they were beyond help. She remembered him saying, "Look, if I die, I'm doing what I like. There's nothing you can do." Now, in a foreign country, with Hopkins failing, the weather bad and no help in sight, she thought it was playing out exactly like her worst fears.

At two P.M., Sakalova returned in the truck. She carried a bag fitted to a tube with a hose clamp. She had Hopkins

Hopkins with his students, Julie Brigham-Grette (left) and Patricia Heiser, and Russians Pavel Ivanov and Dr. Vladimir Pushkar, Nunyamaveyem Bluff, Chukotka, 1992
*(Photo courtesy of Dana Hopkins)*

breathe its contents, which she said was oxygen. By four-thirty it was clear that no helicopter was coming, so Hopkins agreed to accompany the woman back to her village. The group decided that Brigham-Grette would stay and finish the fieldwork, while Patricia Heiser would accompany Hopkins back to the States. After tearful good-bys, Hopkins and Heiser departed, the big truck knocking its occupants around as it jounced over the tundra.

Another call went out to Providenya saying that a famous American scientist needed a medical evacuation. The next day, a massive Russian nuclear icebreaker hove into view and anchored well offshore. The sea was still too rough for the ship's launch. But the following day, its crew braved the crashing seas and landed at Enmelen to pick up Hopkins and Heiser. The sailors installed Hopkins on a bench in the pilothouse of the launch and charged into the waves. "The waves were incredible," as Brigham-Grette heard the story. "They threw the boat around, left and right, left and right. And when they finally got up to the side of the ice-breaker, the waves were smashing this little boat into the ship. The bench Dave was lying on broke, and he was thrown across the floor. It was really rough and noisy and scary." It looked like he might die on the brink of rescue.

Hopkins reached successively better equipped hospitals in Providenya, Nome, and finally Fairbanks, his home, where his doctor concluded that he had had a mild heart attack. He underwent a number of treatments, which culminated in triple bypass surgery. Jeanne Schaaf remembers visiting Hopkins in the hospital in Anchorage after one of his procedures. She had slipped in after visiting hours, and the recovery ward was dark and quiet. The patients were visible only as dim shapes on the beds, and Schaaf wondered how she would to be able to pick out Hopkins. She began to doubt whether she should be bothering him at all. "And then I notice at the end of the line a spot of bright light. Dave's down there. After these procedures, you can't sit up, you have to stay pretty flat. And he's lying in there flat with bright lights on and he had this array of papers all around his bed. And he was just actively reaching as far as he could to get this and that, working very hard and energetically in complete contrast to the rest of the patients on the ward."

At his dialysis session in Fairbanks, Hopkins' voice is feeble and hoarse, but his soundless laughter is no less merry. I ask him about the episode in Khabarovsk where the Russians chanted his name. He says he can't remember much. He does remember sitting next to General Secretary Vitautus Kontrimavichus, who was hosting the conference. In a whisper, he says, "He told me that the conference arose out of my land bridge book. He also told me that the book had been very influential in the Soviet Union, that it had made many young scientists aware of the possibility of working in interdisciplinary areas, of handling several disciplines. That's one of the most flattering things that has ever been told to me."

Hopkins' connection with the Russians was special, says his friend Andrei Sher. "To say that he was an enthusiastic promoter of close Soviet-American cooperation in the Beringian studies is true and correct, but that is to say nothing about Dave. His passion to science was great, and knowledge immense, but I believe that his unique personality weighed much more, especially in his contacts with me and other Russians during the hard times of the Cold War. He was the only foreigner I knew who tried all the time to think about our lives in that brilliant cage." In 1966, when Sher was a student in the Soviet Union, he says he wrote Hopkins to ask whether fossil Ice Age mammals had yet been discovered in Beringia. Hopkins answered that nothing had been found so far, but, he wrote, "I will gladly bet a bottle of Bourbon against a bottle of vodka that interesting mammals await discovery in Chukotka and Seward Peninsula." "Curiously enough," says Sher, "the first early Pleistocene Beringian mammals were collected just a month later on the Kolyma Lowland and almost at the same time on Seward Peninsula. Since that letter, for 35 years, Dave was my teacher, my example, my conscience, my hope, and one of my best friends on both continents."

Lots of scientists—many of them mentored by Hopkins—say similar things.

—We Arctic and Beringian specialists always keep in mind that there would be no coherent concept of Beringia as a distinctive geographic area and ecosystem if Dave had not established the whole idea of Beringia by decades of arduous physical and intellectual effort. He is a true pioneer—he established an entire field of study.

—One of the most illustrious scientific careers the [U.S. Geological] Survey ever had.

—His research and leadership perfectly embody the interdisciplinary perspective.

—The trend to develop a holistic understanding of our past is one of the most exciting areas of knowledge to develop during this century. ... Hopkins has been an important part of this process.

—Hopkins was and still is the ideal mentor. His shared passion for the Arctic and the people who are a part of that landscape has shaped the direction of Arctic science for generations to come. No one today comes even close to filling his shoes.

—He was, and remains, one of the last great natural historians.

By the time Dave Hopkins had retired from more than fifty years as a field geologist, he had won the U.S. Geological Survey's Outstanding Performance Award and its Special Achievement Award, and he was promoted to the agency's "Super Scientist" pay grade (GS-16). He won the Franklin Burr Award from the National Geographic Society, the A.I. Levorsen Award from the American Association of Petroleum Geologists, the Roald Fryxel Award for Interdisciplinary Research from the Society for American Antiquity, the Career Award in Distinguished Quaternary Studies from the American Quaternary Association; and from the Geological Society of

America, the Quaternary Geology and Geomorphology Division's Distinguished Career Award, its Kirk Bryan Award, and the Archeology Division's Distinguished Career Award. The University of Alaska Fairbanks awarded him an honorary Doctor of Science in 2000. The citation noted, "David Hopkins is the person most widely considered responsible for developing the geologic concept of Beringia."

In his curriculum vitae, under a heading he called "Vanity Item," Hopkins lists several extinct species (discovered as fossils) that have been named in his honor. They are not the mighty cats, bears, and elephants commonly associated with ancient Beringia (those having been named already), but include, in ascending order of ferocity, a willow, a shrub rose, a cockleshell, a barnacle, a beetle, and a lemming.

Likely, the most enduring tribute to Hopkins' research was the creation of the Bering Land Bridge National Preserve, a unit of the U.S. National Park System. In the early 1970s, a Park Service planner from San Francisco named John Reynolds looked at northern Seward Peninsula for lands that might warrant selection under what later would be called the Alaska National Interest Lands Act of 1980. Reynolds thought that the Lost Jim lava flows and the Devil Mountain maars were interesting. But when he visited Dave Hopkins, he began to see the landscape as layered with a multitude of meanings. "The result," says Reynolds, "was we went from a pretty well-researched study to a study that was informed by a man who knew in depth about the interrelationships between time and sea level and people's movements and vegetation and animals. I think more than anybody else he's responsible for putting the concept of the whole park proposal together, that included volcanism and biology and paleobotany and the succession of different tundra types and intertwining all of that with the movement of people into North America. I mean, he was an absolute inspiration." Today, Reynolds oversees all the national parks in California, Oregon, Nevada, Idaho, Hawaii, Guam, Saipan, and American Samoa. In connection with his job, he visits some pretty spectacular landscapes. "In truth, Bering Land Bridge is my favorite national park in the whole world," he says, "partly because it taught me about conservation biology, but also because it taught me about the layers." Set aside to teach and inspire, the 2.7-million-acre remnant of the ancient land bridge also stands as a monument to the fifty years of scientific work accomplished there by Dave Hopkins.

Perhaps the professional legacy most meaningful to Hopkins is his intellectual progeny. He is particularly known for assisting the professional development of women scientists, several of whom (like Drs. Julie Brigham-Grette and Patricia Heiser) are established Beringian scholars today. Another of Hopkin's intellectual daughters was also a genetic one. When his children were small, Hopkins took them on walks along San Francisquito Creek, a rivulet that runs down the east side of the Santa Cruz Mountains, through Menlo Park and out into San Francisco Bay. He showed them the preferences of the flowers, the habits of the frogs, and the recondite story of the rocks. He opened up to them the natural history of the world, as his mother, Hebe, had done for him, as her Aunt Nell had done for her. In all three of the children Hopkins enkindled a love of the outdoors, but his middle child, Chindi, was affected in the way that he had been. Her growing interest in the scientific explanations of nature prompted Hopkins to bring her along as a field assistant to Seward Peninsula in 1970 when she was sixteen. That was all it took. Chindi went on to earn bachelor's, master's, and doctorate degrees in, respectively, biology, pathobiology, and parasitology. Today, she works as a

Hopkins' daughters Dana and Chindi explore the margins of a stream in 1961 *(Photo courtesy of Dana Hopkins)*

vector ecologist, studying the transmission of diseases like West Nile Virus. When Chindi took her own daughter into the woods, she continued a family tradition that extended back for over one hundred years for five generations.

Looking back on Dave Hopkins' life is like watching a film scrolling backward: A legendary scholar rises, rumpled and bent, from the banquet table. Accepting an award, he delivers a speech studded with tales told at his own expense, as well as pointed admonitions and challenges. A popular professor, kindly and avuncular, guides a graduate seminar, offering more questions than answers, slyly training his students to supersede him. A rugged field scientist jumps impatiently from the pontoon of a float plane at the edge of a wilderness lake, eager to set up camp, thrilled with the prospect of fieldwork in a wild landscape. At the western edge of the continent, an aspiring young scholar huddles against the mists, shielding his field notebook as he sifts his thoughts and composes a letter to his parents. On a perfect spring day, a small boy bursts into the bright New Hampshire sunshine, running across the yard as the screen door bangs behind him. Bang again, he's back in the kitchen, skidding to a stop, grabbing his knapsack. Bang and he is out of the yard, over the wall, tearing across the field to Gypson's Woods. He moves through green woods, through leaf-dappled light, without apparent plan, finding starflowers and trillium, jack-in-the-pulpit and sweet fern. On his belly beside a cool-running brook, he lifts a string of toads' eggs, dripping and flashing like treasure. Leaning against the kitchen doorframe, his young mother dries her hands on her apron and watches him disappear into the thicket. For a while, she lingers there as if she could see him still. He is crossing the stream. Stone to stone. Happily exploring. Happily putting the world together. Granite, trillium, and toad. Cellar holes and Indian trails. She smiles. Pleased. Well pleased.

# AFTERWORD

For health reasons, and to be nearer their children and grandchildren, Dave and Rachel Hopkins moved back to Menlo Park, California, in the summer of 1999. In late October 2001, after this manuscript was written, but before it was published, Dave suffered a number of medical setbacks. He elected to discontinue dialysis, knowing that it meant he would have only a week or two to live. As word spread, friends called from all over the world to tell him what an inspiration he had been, what an honor it had been to be his friend. For those working in the learned occupations, Hopkins' life had been a model, marked by his intrepid curiosity, his interest in and mastery of an astonishing array of subjects, his subordination of ego to the advancement of knowledge, his sense of public service, his mentoring of students and protégés. He had not only added importantly to our understanding of the world, he'd taught us a lot about how to live.

Part of the time, Dave seemed to know exactly what was happening, but he frequently slipped into periods of delightful confusion. As his daughter Dana said, "His mind is all over the place, but in neat places." When I called from Fairbanks, he at first thought I was at the door to his apartment building, phoning to be buzzed in. I tried to explain, but he said, "Well then why don't you jump in your jalopy and come on over?" I said again that I was at home, in Alaska. He said with anticipation, "I should be going home at the end of the week." Once, say his children, he stood unsteadily in the living room, pointing to the wall, annotating the geological strata revealed there in the icy cutbank. When his kids tried to coax him into sitting on the couch, he refused until they began referring to the couch as a cot, so joining him at his field camp.

A little while later, Dave went home as he planned. He lies in the little cemetery in Greenfield, with Joan on one side and a place for Rachael on the other.

His friend Andrei Sher offered these words to Hopkins' friends, assembled at a memorial service: "Beringia—a huge land that in the nearest past joined together the Old and New Worlds, Eurasia and America, Russia and USA, Siberia and Alaska—was used to giants. Those big woollies—they wandered from one world to another, transferring and spreading their skills, knowledge and personal experience to the rest of the world as a genetic contribution to the Evolution of Life. Most of them died out about ten thousand years ago. The last giant of Beringia, Dave Hopkins, died on Friday, November 2, 2001."

One day, shortly before he became bedridden, Hopkins accompanied his daughter to meet her son at school. Coincidentally, the boy's seventh grade class had been studying the land bridge and knew about Hopkins, knew him as the superstar of Beringian science. When he entered the room, and the teacher told the kids who he was, they burst into a spontaneous cheer. As happened in the midst of another collection of scholars in Siberia many years earlier, this group also clamored for a few words from the honored visitor. And though any recollection of the Soviet scientists chanting his name had faded from Hopkins' memory, this acclamation, no doubt equally valued, took its place in his memory during his last days.

# Bibliographic Notes

**Note on Sources**

Dr. William Schneider, curator of oral history at the University of Alaska, conducted a number of oral history interviews with Dave Hopkins between 1984 and 1994. Sometimes Schneider was joined by other interviewers. I recorded interviews with Dave in 1986 and 1989. Copies of the tape recordings, most of which are transcribed in rough draft form, are available in the Oral History Collection, Alaska and Polar Regions Department, Rasmuson Library, University of Alaska Fairbanks. Hopkins has donated more than twenty boxes of as yet unorganized and unaccessioned papers to the same repository. Of particular use to me were the field notebooks, the correspondence file (filed by correspondent), the correspondence with family members (roughly grouped by year), his correspondence with Louis Giddings, and his file of published and unpublished writing (which he had labeled the "Narcissus File"). In addition to archival sources, I interviewed Hopkins many times, in person and over the telephone, between 1998 and 2001. These interviews were not tape-recorded. A list of Dave Hopkins' two-hundred-odd publications can be found at *http://alaska.usgs.gov/geology/d.hopkins.biblio*.

**1. The toast of Khabarovsk**

Dawson, George M. "Geological Notes on Some of the Coasts and Islands of Bering Sea and Vicinity," *Geological Society of America Bulletin*, Vol. 5, 1894.

Dixon, E. James. *Quest for the Origins of the First Americans.* University of New Mexico Press, 1993.

Dixon, E. James. Telephone interview, 12 December 1998.

Elias, S. A. and J. Brigham-Grette, eds. "Beringian Paleoenvironments Festschrift in Honor of D. M. Hopkins," *Quaternary Science Reviews*, Vol. 20, Nos. 1–3, Pergamon, January 2001.

Hopkins, David M. Interviewed by author, various dates.

David M. Hopkins Collection, Alaska and Polar Regions Collections, Rasmuson Library, University of Alaska Fairbanks. See especially the field notebooks and correspondence with parents.

Hopkins, David M., ed. *The Bering Land Bridge*. Stanford University Press, 1967.

**2. The Ice Age**

Dixon, E. James. *Quest for the Origins of the First Americans.* University of New Mexico Press, 1993.

Elias, Scott A. *The Ice Age History of Alaska National Parks.* Smithsonian Institution Press, 1995.

Elias, S. A. and J. Brigham-Grette, eds. "Beringian Paleoenvironments Festschrift in Honor of D. M. Hopkins," *Quaternary Science Reviews*, Vol. 20, Nos. 1–3, Pergamon, January 2001.

Fagan, Brian M. *The Great Journey: The Peopling of Ancient America*. Thames and Hudson, 1987.

Guthrie, R. Dale. *Frozen Fauna of the Mammoth Steppe*. University of Chicago Press, 1990.

Guthrie, Russell D. "Re-creating a Vanished World," *National Geographic*, Vol. 141 (3).

Haag, William G. "The Bering Strait Land Bridge," in Richard S. MacNeish, ed., *Early Man in America: Readings from Scientific American*. W. H. Freeman and Company, 1973.

David M. Hopkins Collection, Alaska and Polar Regions Collections, Rasmuson Library, University of Alaska Fairbanks. See especially the book reviews file.

Hopkins, David M. Oral history interviews conducted by William Schneider and Dan O'Neill, various dates; Oral History Collection, Alaska and Polar Regions Department, Rasmuson Library, University of Alaska Fairbanks.

Hopkins, David M. "Cenozoic History of the Bering Land Bridge," *Science*, Vol. 129, June 5, 1959.

Hopkins, David M., ed. *The Bering Land Bridge*. Stanford University Press, 1967.

Meltzer, David J. *Search for the First Americans*. Smithsonian Books, 1993.

**3. Hebe's son**

Hopkins, David M. Interviewed by author; various dates.

Hopkins, David M. Oral history interviews conducted by William Schneider and Dan O'Neill, various dates; Oral History Collection, Alaska and Polar Regions Department, Rasmuson Library, University of Alaska Fairbanks.

Hopkins, Henrietta M. and Ruth W. Ledward. *A Brief History of Greenfield, New Hampshire, 1791–1941*. Apparently published by the General Committee of the Sesquicentennial Celebration of Greenfield's founding, Greenfield, New Hampshire, 1941.

Hopkins, Doris E. *Greenfield, N.H.: The Story of a Town, 1791–1976*. Wallace Press, Milford, New Hampshire, 1977.

**4. Calling**

Hopkins, David M. Interviewed by author, various dates.

Hopkins, David M. Oral history interviews conducted by William Schneider and Dan O'Neill, various dates; Oral History Collection, Alaska and Polar Regions Department, Rasmuson Library, University of Alaska Fairbanks.

David M. Hopkins Collection, Alaska and Polar Regions Collections, Rasmuson Library, University of Alaska Fairbanks. See especially the correspondence with parents.

**5. Fieldwork in arctic Alaska**

Constance, Lincoln, "Plants in Beringia," book review in *Science*, October 25, 1968.

David M. Hopkins Collection, Alaska and Polar Regions Collections, Rasmuson Library, University of Alaska Fairbanks. See especially the correspondence with parents, field notebooks.

Hopkins, David M. Oral history interviews conducted by William Schneider and Dan O'Neill, various dates; Oral History Collection, Alaska and Polar Regions Department, Rasmuson Library, University of Alaska Fairbanks.

David M. Hopkins. "The Bering Land Bridge—Early Research," *Ublasaun* (First Light): *Inupiaq Hunters and Herders in the Early Twentieth Century, Northern Seward Peninsula, Alaska*. National Park Service, 1996.

Hopkins, David M. "Thaw Lakes and Thaw Sinks in the Imuruk Lake Area, Seward Peninsula, Alaska," *Journal of Geology*, Vol. 57, 1949.

Hopkins, David M. "History of Imuruk Lake, Seward Peninsula, Alaska," *Geological Society of America Bulletin*, Vol. 70, 1959.

Hultén, Eric, *Outline of the History of Arctic and Boreal Biota During the Quaternary Period*, Strauss und Cramer, Germany, 1937. Reprint of the Stockholm edition, 1937.

Hultén, Eric. *Flora of Alaska and Neighboring Territories*. Stanford University Press, 1968.

Hultén, Eric. *Autobiography*. Undated manuscript in David M. Hopkins Collection, University of Alaska Fairbanks Archives.

Hultén, Eric. *Men Roligt har det Varit: En Forskares Memoarer*. Generalstabens Lithografiska Anstalts Förlag, Stockholm, 1973.

Larsen, Helge. "Trail Creek: Final Report on the Excavation of Two Caves on Seward Peninsula, Alaska," *Acta Arctica*, Fasc. XV. Ejnar Munksgaard, Kobenhavn; 1968.

Love, Askell. "Eric Hultén: 1894–1981, In Memoriam," obituary in *Arctic, Antarctic and Alpine Research* (formerly *Arctic and Alpine Research*), Vol. 13, No. 13, August 1981.

Murray, David. F., Sylvia Kelso, and Boris A. Yurtsev. "Floristic Novelties in Beringia: Patterns and Questions of Their Origins," in *Bridges of Science Between North America and the Russian Far East: Proceedings of the 45th Arctic Science Conference*, August 25–27, 1994, Anchorage, Alaska and August 29–September 2, 1994, Vladivostock, Russia.

**6. Something going on**

Hopkins, David M. Interviewed by author, various dates.

Hopkins, David M. Oral history interviews conducted by William Schneider and Dan O'Neill, various dates; Oral

History Collection, Alaska and Polar Regions Department, Rasmuson Library, University of Alaska Fairbanks.

David M. Hopkins Collection, Alaska and Polar Regions Collections, Rasmuson Library, University of Alaska Fairbanks. See especially the correspondence with parents.

**7. Giddings**

——. Obituary of J. L. Giddings in *Polar Record*, Vol. 66, No. 82, January 1966.

Collins, Henry B. Obituary of J. L. Giddings in *Arctic*, Vol. 18, No. 1, March 1965.

Dayton, Paul. E-mail correspondence with author, 2000. Dayton is Louis Giddings' nephew and worked with him in the field.

Giddings, J. Louis. *Ancient Men of the Arctic*. Knopf, 1967.

Giddings, J. Louis. "Early Man in the Arctic;" in Richard S. MacNeish, ed., *Early Man in America*. W. H. Freeman, 1973.

David M. Hopkins Collection, Alaska and Polar Regions Collections, Rasmuson Library, University of Alaska Fairbanks. See especially the correspondence with Giddings, correspondence with parents, field notebooks.

Hopkins, David M. Oral history interviews conducted by William Schneider and Dan O'Neill, various dates; Oral History Collection, Alaska and Polar Regions Department, Rasmuson Library, University of Alaska Fairbanks.

Hopkins, D. M. and J. L. Giddings. *Geological Background of the Iyatayet Archeological Site, Cape Denbigh, Alaska.* Smithsonian Institution, 1953.

Larsen, Helge. "Trail Creek: Final Report on the Excavation of Two Caves on Seward Peninsula, Alaska," in *Acta Arctica*, Fasc. XV. Ejnar Munksgaard, Kobenhavn; 1968.

Nash, Stephen E. "James Louis Giddings' Archeological Tree-ring Dating in the American Arctic: A Forgotten Legacy," *Arctic Anthropology*, Vol. 37, No. 1, 2000, pp. 60–78, 2000.

**8. A simultaneous equation**

Elias, Scott A., Susan Short, C. Hans Nelson, and Hillary Birks. "Life and Times of the Bering Land Bridge," *Nature*, Vol. 382, July 4, 1996.

Fagan, Brian M. *The Great Journey: The Peopling of Ancient America*. Thames and Hudson, 1987.

David M. Hopkins Collection, Alaska and Polar Regions Collections, Rasmuson Library, University of Alaska Fairbanks. See especially the field notebooks.

Hopkins, David M. Oral history interviews conducted by William Schneider and Dan O'Neill, various dates; Oral History Collection, Alaska and Polar Regions Department, Rasmuson Library, University of Alaska Fairbanks.

Hopkins, David M., *The Bering Land Bridge*. Stanford University Press, 1967.

Hopkins, David M., J. V. Matthews, C. E. Schweger, and S. B. Young. *Paleoecology of Beringia*. Academic Press, 1982.

Marincovich, Louie, Jr. and Andrey Yu. Gladenkov. "Evidence for an Early Opening of Bering Strait," *Nature*, Vol. 397, January 14, 1999.

Marincovich, Louie, Jr., Elisabeth M. Brouwers, David M. Hopkins, and Malcolm C. McKenna. "Late Mesozoic and Cenozoic Paleographic and Paleoclimatic History of the Arctic Ocean Basin, Based on Shallow-water Marine Faunas and Terrestrial Vertebrates," in *The Geology of North America*, Vol. L, *The Arctic Ocean Region*. The Geological Society of America, 1990.

Marincovich, Louie, Jr. E-mail correspondence with author, 2000.

Oquilluk, William A, with Laurel L. Bland. *People of Kauwerak: Legends of the Northern Eskimo*. Alaska Methodist University Press, 1973.

Repenning, Charles A. E-mail correspondence with author, 2000.

Repenning, Charles A. "Palearctic-Neararctic Mammalian Dispersal in the Late Cenozoic," in David M. Hopkins, ed. *The Bering Land Bridge*. Stanford University Press, 1967.

Sher, Andrei. "Traffic Lights at the Beringian Crossroads," *Nature*, Vol. 397, January 1999, pp. 103–104.

**9. Writing the bible**

Creager, Joe S. and Dean A. McManus. "Geology of the Floor of Bering and Chukchi Seas—American Studies," in David M. Hopkins, ed. *The Bering Land Bridge*. Stanford University Press, 1967.

Hopkins, David M. *The Bering Land Bridge*. Stanford University Press, 1967.

David M. Hopkins Collection, Alaska and Polar Regions Collections, Rasmuson Library, University of Alaska Fairbanks. See especially the field notebooks.

Hopkins, David M. Oral history interviews conducted by William Schneider and Dan O'Neill, various dates; Oral History Collection, Alaska and Polar Regions Department, Rasmuson Library, University of Alaska Fairbanks.

Repenning, Charles A. E-mail correspondence with author, 2000.

Repenning, Charles A. "Palearctic-Neararctic Mammalian Dispersal in the Late Cenozoic," in David M. Hopkins, ed. *The Bering Land Bridge*. Stanford University Press, 1967.

Scholl, David W. and David M. Hopkins. "Newly Discovered Cenozoic Basins, Bering Sea Shelf, Alaska," *The American*

*Association of Geologists Bulletin*, Vol. 53, No. 10 October, 1969, pp. 2067–2078.

Scholl, David W., Edwin C. Buffington, David M. Hopkins, and Tau Rho Alpha. "The Structure and Origin of the Large Submarine Canyons of the Bering Sea," *Marine Geology*, Vol. 8, 1970, pp. 187–210.

**10. The productivity paradox**

Colinvaux, Paul A. and Fredrick H. West. "The Beringian Ecosystem," *The Quarterly Review of Archeology*, September 1984.

Colinvaux, Paul A. "Plain Thinking on Bering Land Bridge Vegetation and Mammoth Populations," *The Quarterly Review of Archeology*, March 1986.

Fagan, Brian M. *The Great Journey: The Peopling of Ancient America*, Thames and Hudson, 1987.

Guthrie, R. D. and John V. Matthews. "The Cape Deceit Fauna—Early Pleistocene Mammalian Assemblage from the Alaskan Arctic," *Quaternary Research*, Vol. 1, 1971.

Guthrie, R. Dale. "Woolly Arguments Against the Mammoth Steppe—A New Look at the Palynological Data," *The Quarterly Review of Archeology*, September 1985.

Guthrie, R. Dale. *Frozen Fauna of the Mammoth Steppe*. University of Chicago Press, 1990.

Hopkins, David M., J. V. Matthews, C. E. Schweger, and S. B. Young. *Paleoecology of Beringia*. Academic Press, 1982.

David M. Hopkins Collection, Alaska and Polar Regions Collections, Rasmuson Library, University of Alaska Fairbanks. See especially the field notebooks.

Hopkins, David M. Oral history interviews conducted by William Schneider and Dan O'Neill, various dates; Oral

History Collection, Alaska and Polar Regions Department, Rasmuson Library, University of Alaska Fairbanks.

Matthews, J. V., Jr. "Quaternary Environments at Cape Deceit (Seward Peninsula, Alaska): Evolution of a Tundra Ecosystem," *Geological Society of America Bulletin*, Vol. 85, September 1974.

Meltzer, David J. *Search for the First Americans*. Smithsonian Books, 1993.

**11. Mammoth fauna**

Colinvaux, Paul A. and Fredrick H. West. "The Beringian Ecosystem," *The Quarterly Review of Archeology*, September 1984.

Colinvaux, Paul A. "Plain Thinking on Bering Land Bridge Vegetation and Mammoth Populations," *The Quarterly Review of Archeology*, March 1986.

Colinvaux, Paul A. "Low-down on the Land Bridge," *Nature*, Vol. 382, July 4, 1996.

Colinvaux, Paul A., Dan A. Livingstone, and David M. Hopkins. "Reconnaissance of Large Lakes in the Proposed Imuruk-Chukchi Wildlands to Consider Possibility and Desirability of Lifting Long Cores," unpublished and undated manuscript, David M. Hopkins Collection, Alaska and Polar Regions Collections, Rasmuson Library, University of Alaska Fairbanks.

Elias, Scott A. *The Ice Age History of Alaska National Parks*. Smithsonian Institution Press, 1995.

Elias, Scott A., Susan Short, C. Hans Nelson, and Hillary Birks. "Life and Times of the Bering Land Bridge," *Nature*, Vol. 382, July 4, 1996.

Guthrie, R. Dale. *Frozen Fauna of the Mammoth Steppe*. University of Chicago Press, 1990.

Guthrie, R. D. and John V. Matthews. "The Cape Deceit Fauna—Early Pleistocene Mammalian Assemblage from the Alaskan Arctic," *Quaternary Research*, Vol. 1, 1971.

Guthrie, R. Dale. "Woolly Arguments Against the Mammoth Steppe—A New Look at the Palynological Data," *The Quarterly Review of Archeology*, September 1985.

David M. Hopkins Collection, Alaska and Polar Regions Collections, Rasmuson Library, University of Alaska Fairbanks. See especially the field notebooks.

Hopkins, David M. Oral history interviews conducted by William Schneider, Dan O'Neill, and others, various dates; Oral History Collection, Alaska and Polar Regions Department, Rasmuson Library, University of Alaska Fairbanks.

Hopkins, David M., J. V. Matthews, C. E. Schweger, and S. B. Young. *Paleoecology of Beringia*. Academic Press, 1982.

Matthews, J. V., Jr. "Quaternary Environments at Cape Deceit (Seward Peninsula, Alaska): Evolution of a Tundra Ecosystem," *Geological Society of America Bulletin*, Vol. 85, September 1974.

U.S. National Park Service, Shared Beringian Heritage Program, Alaska Support Office. *Journey of Discovery: Landscape History of the Bering Land Bridge*. Video recording produced by Taylor Productions, Inc., undated.

U.S. National Park Service, Shared Beringian Heritage Program, Alaska Support Office. *Siulipta Paitaat: Our Ancestors' Heritage*. Video recording produced by Taylor Productions, Inc., undated.

Wood, Charles A. and Jürgen Kienle. *Volcanoes of North America: United States and Canada*. Cambridge University Press, 1993.

**12. Soil from maars**

Colinvaux, Paul A., Dan A. Livingstone, and David M. Hopkins. "Reconnaissance of Large Lakes in the Proposed Imuruk-Chukchi Wildlands to Consider Possibility and Desirability of Lifting Long Cores." Unpublished and undated manuscript, David M. Hopkins Collection, Alaska and Polar Regions Collections, Rasmuson Library, University of Alaska Fairbanks.

Goetcheus, Victoria G., Jan Janssens, and David M. Hopkins. "The Vegetation of A17 Buried Surface on the Northern Seward Peninsula," Arctic Workshop, 24th, Quebec, Abstracts, 1995.

Goetcheus, Victoria G. "Reconstruction of a Full Glacial Landscape Based on Macrofossils," Quaternary Geology/Geomorphology (Posters II), Session 119, Annual Meeting, Denver, 1996, *Geological Society of America Abstracts with Programs*, Vol. 28, No. 7, p. A-303.

Goetcheus, Victoria G. and Hilary H. Birks. "Full-Glacial Upland Tundra Vegetation Preserved under Tephra in the Beringia National Park, Seward Peninsula, Alaska," unpublished, undated manuscript.

Hopkins, David M. "The Espenberg Maars: A Record of Explosive Volcanic Activity in the Devil Mountain-Cape Espenberg Area, Seward Peninsula, Alaska," in *The Bering Land Bridge National Preserve: An Archeological Survey*, J. Schaaf, National Park Service, Alaska Region Research/Management Report AR-14, 1988.

David M. Hopkins Collection, Alaska and Polar Regions Collections, Rasmuson Library, University of Alaska Fairbanks. See especially the field notebooks.

Hopkins, David M. Oral history interviews conducted by William Schneider, Dan O'Neill, and others, various dates;

Oral History Collection, Alaska and Polar Regions Department, Rasmuson Library, University of Alaska Fairbanks.

Hopkins, David M. Interviewed by author, various dates.

Höfle, Claudia. *Buried Soils on Seward Peninsula, Northwest Alaska: A Window into the Late-Pleistocene Environment of the Bering Land Bridge*. Masters thesis, University of Alaska Fairbanks, August 1995.

Wolf, Victoria Goetcheus. *A Window to the Past: Macrofossil Remains from an 18,000 Year-old Surface, Seward Peninsula, Alaska.* Masters thesis, University of Alaska Fairbanks, December, 2001.

Wood, Charles A. and Jürgen Kienle. *Volcanoes of North America: United States and Canada.* Cambridge University Press, 1993.

**13. The first Americans**

———. Obituary of J. L. Giddings in *Polar Record*, Vol. 66, No. 82, January 1966.

———. "Brown Professor Badly Hurt in Seekonk Highway Crash" and "Auto Injuries Prove Fatal to Dr. Giddings," undated (probably December 1964), unattributed newspaper clippings. Provided by Bruce Crooks, Haffenreffer Museum of Anthropology, Brown University, Bristol, Rhode Island.

Anderson, Douglas. Telephone interview, April 6, 2000. Anderson was Giddings' student and completed the excavations begun by Giddings at Onion Portage.

Anderson, Douglas. "Onion Portage: The Archeology of a Stratified Site from the Kobuk River, Northwest Alaska," *Anthropological Papers of the University of Alaska*, Vol. 22, Nos. 1–2, 1986.

Carlisle, Kate. E-mail correspondence with author, 2000. Carlisle is Giddings' niece and was a student at Brown at the time of her uncle's death.

Collins, Henry B. Obituary of J. L. Giddings in *Arctic*, Vol. 18, No. 1, March 1965.

Dayton, Paul. E-mail correspondence with author, 2000. Dayton is Louis Giddings' nephew and worked with him in the field.

Dixon, E. James. *Quest for the Origins of the First Americans*. University of New Mexico Press, 1993.

Dixon, E. James. *Bones, Boats and Bison: Archeology and the First Colonists of Western North America*. University of New Mexico Press, 1999.

Elias, Scott A. *The Ice Age History of Alaska National Parks*. Smithsonian Institution Press, 1995.

Fagan, Brian M. *The Great Journey: The Peopling of Ancient America*. Thames and Hudson, 1987.

Giddings, J. Louis. *Ancient Men of the Arctic*. Knopf, 1967.

Greenberg, Joseph H., Christy G. Turner II, and Stephen L. Zegura. "The Settlement of the Americas: A Comparison of the Linguistic, Dental, and Genetic Evidence," *Current Anthropology*, Vol. 27, No. 5, December 1986.

Greenberg, Joseph H. "Beringia and New World Origins: The Linguistic Evidence," in F. H. West, ed., *American Beginnings*, University of Chicago Press, 1996.

Hamilton, Thomas D. and Ted Goebel. "Late Pleistocene Peopling of Alaska," in R. Bonnichsen and K. L. Turnmire, eds., *Ice Age Peoples of North America*. Oregon State University Press, 1999.

Hopkins, David M. *The Bering Land Bridge*. Stanford University Press, 1967.

David M. Hopkins Collection, Alaska and Polar Regions Collections, Rasmuson Library, University of Alaska Fairbanks. See especially the field notebooks.

Hopkins, David M. Oral history interviews conducted by William Schneider, Dan O'Neill, and others, various dates; Oral History Collection, Alaska and Polar Regions Department, Rasmuson Library, University of Alaska Fairbanks.

Laughlin, William S. and Albert B. Harper, eds. *The First Americans: Origins, Affinities, and Adaptations*. Gustav Fischer, 1979.

Laughlin, William S. "Human Migration and Permanent Occupation in the Bering Sea Area," in David M. Hopkins, ed. *The Bering Land Bridge*, Stanford University Press, 1967.

Meltzer, David J. *Search for the First Americans*. Smithsonian Books, 1993.

Turner, Christy G. "Teeth and Prehistory in Asia," *Scientific American*, February 1989.

Turner, Christy G. *The Dentition of Arctic Peoples*. Garland, 1991.

Thomas, David Hurst. *Skull Wars: Kennewick Man, Archeology, and the Battle for Native American Identity*. Basic Books, 2000.

West, Fredrick H., ed. *American Beginnings: The Prehistory and Paleoecology of Beringia*. University of Chicago Press, 1996.

**14. The first of the first**

Dixon, E. James. *Quest for the Origins of the First Americans*. University of New Mexico Press, 1993.

Dixon, E. James. *Bones, Boats and Bison: Archeology and the First Colonists of Western North America.* University of New Mexico Press, 1999.

Meltzer, David J. *Search for the First Americans.* Smithsonian Books, 1993.

Mobley, Charles M. *The Campus Site: A Prehistoric Camp at Fairbanks, Alaska.* University of Alaska Press, 1991.

Rainey, Froelich. "Louis Giddings: Obituary; American Anthropologist," Vol. 67, No. 6, Pt. 1, December 1965.

West, Fredrick H., ed. *American Beginnings: The Prehistory and Paleoecology of Beringia.* University of Chicago Press, 1996.

Workman, William. To author, January 6, 2001.

**15. The last of the last**

Brigham-Grette, Julie. E-mail to author, May 16, 2001; telephone interview, May 3, 2001.

Hamilton, Thomas. Oral history interview, January 6, 2001; numerous telephone interviews and e-mails, various dates, 2001.

Hopkins, David M. Interviewed by author, various dates.

Reynolds, John. Telephone interview, May 1, 2001.

Schaaf, Jeanne. Oral history interviews with author, April 1, 1999, September 15, 2000; numerous telephone interviews, 1998–2002.

Sher, Andrei, to Professor Julie Brigham-Grette, November 17, 2001.

Society for American Archeology. 1988 Fryxell Award for Interdisciplinary Research, citation in American Antiquity, 53(3), 1988, pp. 453–454.

Thorson, Robert M. Citation on the presentation of the Archeological Geology Division Award, 1990.

University of Alaska Fairbanks. Citation for David M. Hopkins, honorary doctorate, May 2000.

University of Maine at Orono. Citation for David M. Hopkins, Distinguished Lecture Series, October 1983.

Workman, William, to The Fryxell Award Committee, October 20, 1986.

**Afterword**

Hopkins, Dana. Telephone interviews, November 2001 to February 2002.

Hopkins, David M. Telephone interviews, November. 2001.

Schaaf, Jeanne. Telephone interviews, November 2001.

# Acknowledgments

My friend and colleague, Bill Schneider, curator of oral history at Rasmuson Library, University of Alaska Fairbanks, conceived of this project in the mid-1980s and recorded many interviews with Hopkins over the span of a decade. To this substantial volume of material (all transcribed), I added additional recordings with Hopkins in the 1980s. These oral history recordings served as the core primary source material for this book. I thank especially Jeanne Schaaf of the National Park Service for seeing the value of the project, as well as Dave Spirtes and Peter Richter, for arranging financial support from the Western Arctic Parklands and the Beringia program.

Many people helped me to learn some of the ideas of Beringian science, and any errors herein are due to my failings, not theirs. I thank Paul Matheus, Julie Brigham-Grette, Bill Workman, Dale Guthrie, and Dan Hopkins who read whole manuscript—and especially Tom Hamilton who read it multiple times—their comments improved it significantly. Also helpful to me on the science were Dave Scholl, Nancy Bigelow, Andrea Krumhardt, Owen Mason, Charles Repenning, Louie Marincovich, Charlie Schweger, Dave Murray, and Vicky Goetcheus Wolf. Others gave me biographical information on Hopkins or Giddings: Dan Hopkins, Ginny and Bob Hillegass, Paul Dayton, Kate Carlisle, Jim Dixon, Andrei Sher, Bob Sattler, Parke Snavely, Art Grantz, Art

Lachenbruch, George Gryc, Bob Rowland, Doug Anderson, and Christy Turner. I got excellent support at Rasmuson Library's Alaska and Polar Regions Department at the University of Alaska Fairbanks, especially from Bill Schneider, Marla Statscewich, Karen Brewster, and Carone Sturm at the Oral History Program. Marla saved my bacon a hundred times as I plodded through Photoshop making the maps. Also helpful at Rasmuson Library were Lorrie Boon, Peggy Asbury, Sylvie Savage, Rose Speranza, Gretchen Lake, and Susan Grigg. Judie Triplehorn at UAF's Geophysical Institute's library is a paragon of reference librarianship, one who keeps your research interests filed in her mind and calls you up whenever something interesting crosses her desk. For Giddings material, I thank Rip Gerry and Bruce Crooks at Brown University's Haffenreffer Museum of Anthropology, and Rex Adams of the Laboratory of Tree Ring Research at the University of Arizona. Julie Brigham-Grette gave me important information, comments on the draft, and the use of her excellent photographs. Andrei Sher also kindly scanned and sent me photos. Dave's kids, Chindi Peavey and Dana Hopkins, helped me on several occasions, especially by letting me dig for photographs in Dave's jam-packed storage locker. Brian Peavey kindly helped me sift through that ten-by-ten-by-ten-foot midden. Dave's cousin Ginny and her husband Bob showed my wife and me great hospitality during our visit to Greenfield. The crew at the National Park Service office in Fairbanks, especially Eileen Devinney, Debbie Nigro, Nikki Guldager, and Stacey McIntosh, gave me lots of help scanning images and developing maps. Seth Danielson and Dave Musgrave of the University of Alaska Fairbanks Institute of Marine Science kindly provided bathymetric data. Alan Batten and Les Viereck lent me photos of Eric Hultén and I thank Maj

Hultén for permission to use them. Dave Scholl arranged for me to meet with several senior USGS scientists in Menlo Park. And I thank Kathy and Tom Lynch, Kathleen O'Neill, and Mike and Mary Matza for their hospitality during several trips to Menlo Park.

I was very lucky to have the editorial comments of my nonfiction writer friends: Frank Soos, Sherry Simpson, Jennifer Brice, Gay Salisbury, and Carolyn Kremers. Carolyn read the whole manuscript at a late stage and caught a thousand lapses. I thank my smart, professional, and unfailingly courteous agents, Anna Cottle and Mary Alice Kier of Cine/Lit Representation. At Westview Press, I thank Karl Yambert for seeing the value in the book, Trish Goodrich and Greg Houle for promotion, and Fred Dahl (of Inkwell) for copy editing and for guiding the book production process. My friend Dave Norton kindly volunteered to do the index. Thanks to my wife Sarah and my son Kyle for all the sufferance a book project inflicts. Finally, my greatest debt is to Dave Hopkins, who gave me so many hours of interviews over many years. Dave was a gifted writer, and his suggestions and margin comments always improved the text. Besides all that, in retelling Dave's stories, I frequently favored his phrasing, until he seemed to me at times more coauthor than source. He always wanted to write a memoir along the lines of Louie Giddings' masterpiece *Ancient Men of the Arctic*. By including Dave's stories here—the way he told them—I hope a part of that wish is fulfilled.

# INDEX